Praise for
The Only Negotiating Guide You'll Ever Need

"Your skill as a negotiator determines your success in life. This book provides a wealth of information in an engaging format. Whether you are a new negotiator or a seasoned one, this book is for you!"

—*John Vella, Chief Revenue Officer,*
Altisource Portfolio Solutions

"Without a doubt, the best part of the book is the 101 winning tactics.... So often, people write about theory without demonstrating how theory works—that information is what is truly useful."

—*Mark Guglielmo, Vice President,*
Ballpark Operations, San Diego Padres

"With the ease of access to information [in today's world], a person's negotiation skills are as important as ever. This book has been and is an invaluable resource, and I've happily provided copies to friends and colleagues. The information is straightforward, easily accessible, and applicable to business and personal life."

—*Michael Graves, Sales Manager,*
Residential Wholesale Mortgage, Inc.

"Having readers self-assess their negotiation strengths is brilliant. This got me personally involved in the book. I was encouraged to read more."

—*Tom Koning, Vice President of Sales, BD Medical*

"The reflection on real-life situations gives the book a relevancy that is easy to associate with. [Providing] the process to help [readers] better understand themselves and others equips [them] to be better negotiators."

—*Garry Ridge, President and CEO, WD-40 Company, Inc.*

"Instead of a 'one size fits all' approach, this book acknowledges the reality that situations, and negotiations, differ. In order to negotiate, sell, and just navigate everyday life, one needs to have skill in a variety of tactics (101 tactics, to be precise!)."

—*Marilyn Owsley, Chief Financial Officer,*
SCPMG, Kaiser Permanente

"Believe the title! *The Only Negotiating Guide You'll Ever Need* is required reading for everyone in my organization. Peter and Jane map out how to find win-win solutions and work cooperatively with others. Being able to work with others is the most critical skill a leader can bring to their organization, and Peter and Jane provide tools and tips every leader needs."

—*Mary Kelly, PhD, Commander, USN (ret),*
Consultant/Author

"The title says it all. Excellent resource. Not a one-and-done read, but something you can refer back to over and over again. The principles in this book are not only helpful in business, but in your personal life, too."

—*Mike Dunn, Executive Vice President,*
Watkins Manufacturing

"Whether you are a novice or experienced negotiator, this book will provide the 'how and why' of the tactics for successful negotiations, resulting in adopting the strategy of a Dolphin instead of a Shark."

—*Brad Gessner, Senior Vice President and General*
Manager, Los Angeles Convention Center

"Once in a generation a book comes along that is so concise, so on target, and so practical that it becomes more valuable with time. And that is exactly what *The Only Negotiating Guide You'll Ever Need* is! Get this book into the hands of all of your leadership team and they will immediately improve how your team performs . . . get it into the hands of your sales team and your top line will grow regardless of the market!"

—*Barry Banther, Bestselling Author,* A Leader's Gift:
How to Earn the Right to Be Followed

"Relevant and actionable—thank you for simplifying the complexity around negotiating! This book helped me think and act differently within the first 10 minutes of reading.... Everyone negotiates every day. Therefore, this book is for everyone!"

—*David Horsager, Author, Speaker, and Strategist,*
Trust Edge Leadership Institute

"So much of this book helps us return to good practices in all our dealings with people! Negotiating does not have to be adversarial when you are able to listen carefully to others and let them communicate what is important to them, build trust by being honest (even when it costs you something), and really get to know your negotiating partner and their style and craft a message that works well in communicating specifically with them! Thanks, Peter and Jane, for helping me remember that negotiating well for a win-win is always my ultimate goal."

—*Ellen Schmeding, Director, Aging and Independence*
Services, County of San Diego

"A valuable compilation of easy-to-integrate negotiating skills for business and life. One of the most striking concepts, contrary to the negotiation process that first comes to mind, is that the strong negotiator takes more time to listen than to talk (Chapter 5)."

—*Geri LaChance, President/CEO,*
SESLOC Federal Credit Union

"One of the key challenges facing leaders today is establishing and maintaining engagement with the associates they lead. This book on negotiation serves as a dynamic tool to facilitate mutual engagement, not only with subordinates, but also with peers working toward building a stronger team."

—*Dave Doss, President/CEO, OneAZ Credit Union*

"Over the years, I have used the tactics in this negotiation guide to work with leadership teams, purchase homes, cars, and negotiate compensation packages. By successfully applying the skills I learned through reading this book, I have developed win-win situations and achieved both personal and professional outcomes as a result."

—*Dr. Marie Brown Mercadel, Assistant Director,*
Department of Public Social Services, County of Riverside

"As a General Counsel who is continually negotiating complex and difficult situations, *The Only Negotiation Guide You'll Ever Need* is the go-to resource for designing strategy and tactics to achieve a win-win outcome."

—*Molly Hermann, J.D., CCEP, Vice President, General Counsel, NW Permanente Physicians & Surgeons, P.C.*

"The wisdom of Stark and Flaherty's theories pair seamlessly with practical tactics for negotiation in a way that makes this book an essential part of any professional library. Now more than ever, we need effective tools to help us navigate conflict and challenges. Stark and Flaherty provide this in spades, and I find myself referring to their words in my most critical moments."

—*Doran Barnes, Executive Director, Foothill Transit*

"From the self-assessment of your own negotiating prowess, to the specifics of what makes a successful negotiator, to the presentation of 101 tactics for successful negotiation, this book is an excellent end-to-end tool for developing and enhancing your own and your team's negotiation skills. Success in business is often a game of inches, and the insights provided by this book will give you and your company a much-needed edge in both the small and large transactions you engage in on a daily basis."

—*Terry Shirey, President and COO, Nevada State Bank*

"This book would be extremely beneficial in strengthening negotiation skills. If you are a novice negotiator, this is a succinct vehicle for learning the craft of negotiation. If you are an experienced negotiator, there are good reminders, but also some new thoughts to consider to improve your success rate."

—*Jack Farnan, Senior Consultant, Arete Leadership Group*

THE ONLY NEGOTIATING GUIDE YOU'LL EVER NEED

REVISED AND UPDATED

THE ONLY NEGOTIATING GUIDE YOU'LL EVER NEED

101 WAYS TO WIN EVERY TIME IN ANY SITUATION

REVISED AND UPDATED

Peter B. Stark and Jane Flaherty

CROWN
BUSINESS
NEW YORK

Crown Business books are available at special discounts for bulk purchases for sales promotions or corporate use. Special editions, including personalized covers, excerpts of existing books, or books with corporate logos, can be created in large quantities for special needs. For more information, contact Premium Sales at (212) 572-2232 or e-mail specialmarkets@penguinrandomhouse.com.

Originally self-published in 2002 as *Everyone Negotiates: 101 Winning Tactics*, and subsequently published in the United States by Broadway Books, an imprint of the Crown Publishing Group, a division of Penguin Random House LLC, New York, in 2003.

Library of Congress Cataloging-in-Publication Data
Names: Stark, Peter B., author. | Flaherty, Jane S., author. | Stark, Peter B. Everyone negotiates.
Title: The only negotiating guide you'll ever need, revised and updated : 101 ways to win every time in any situation / Peter B. Stark, Jane Flaherty.
Description: Revised and Updated Edition. | New York : Crown Business, 2017. | Revised edition of The only negotiating guide you'll ever need, 2003.
Identifiers: LCCN 2016044985 | ISBN 9781524758905 (paperback)
Subjects: LCSH: Negotiation. | BISAC: BUSINESS & ECONOMICS / Negotiating. | BUSINESS & ECONOMICS / Motivational. | SELF-HELP / Personal Growth / Success.
Classification: LCC BF637.N4 S725 2017 | DDC 302.3—dc23
LC record available at https://lccn.loc.gov/2016044985

ISBN 978-1-5247-5890-5
Ebook ISBN 978-1-5247-5891-2

Printed in the United States of America

Book design by Christine Welch
Cover design by Darren Haggar

10 9 8 7 6 5 4 3

First Revised Paperback Edition

We have often heard the phrase "Everything is negotiable." Although this sounds true, in fact, some things are not negotiable. On August 17, 1998, Peter's fourteen-year-old daughter and Jane's niece, Brittany, passed away while waiting for a heart transplant. Brittany touched the lives of so many people. She was the type of person who helped us all be the very best parents, sisters, brothers, and friends we could be. Although Brittany's life ended way too soon, we are all blessed to have been a part of it. It seems God needed an angel.

Through the loss of Brittany, we learned the hard way that God's plan is one thing that is not negotiable. Someone once told us, "If you want to make God laugh, share with him 'your' plan."

Brittany, thanks for showing the world what unconditional love, true happiness, and the unwavering courage to fight for what's right look like in real life. Like most teenagers, you were a great negotiator. You were also a wonderful gift to the spirit. This book is dedicated to you. May your dreams live on.

Readers, please sign the organ donor registry and carry your organ donor card. Let your loved ones know you have decided to do so. It is easily done at Donate Life America: https://registerme.org or www.donateLIFEcalifornia.org/brittany. Share your life. It is the last and greatest gift you can give back to God and humanity.

CONTENTS

PART II 101 TACTICS FOR SUCCESSFUL NEGOTIATION AND 20 BONUS TACTICS   129

INTRODUCTION
Why Another Book on Negotiation?

In 2003, *The Only Negotiation Guide You'll Ever Need* was first published. Since its release, the book, e-book, and audio versions have sold close to 100,000 copies. In the last fifteen years, our content and seminars have helped thousands of people become stronger, more confident negotiators. Since the book was first published, we have continued to learn more about negotiation . . . in our personal negotiations, through watching national and international negotiations, and from our seminar participants. As we learned more, we felt compelled to share some of this new knowledge with you, the reader, in our revised, updated edition.

The purpose of this book is to provide you with the skills and tools necessary to be a great negotiator who builds strong, life-long, win-win relationships. The philosophy behind the approach used is that, as a negotiator, you have an obligation to help your counterparts in negotiations come out winners. Why? Because very few negotiations are one-time affairs. With almost every product or service you purchase or sell, even if it's a car or a house, you have the opportunity to build a relationship that will benefit you and strengthen your ability to negotiate all life's outcomes. Think about it. If you are in sales, every negotiation that has a win-win outcome provides you with the opportunity to work with the buyer and the buyer's referrals for the rest of your life. When buying a product or service, most successful people consistently go to contacts they have made in the past win-win negotiations because those connections have resulted in strong relationships based on trust.

You might ask, "But what about buying a car? Isn't that just a one-time negotiation?" Here lies the challenge. For years, car dealerships have treated selling cars as a one-time affair, not bothering to create a pleasant or significant experience for the buyer. As a result, they have left a bad taste in the mouths of car buyers. The reality is that there are some people who have bought two or three cars from the same car dealership and even the same salesperson. This type of relationship is ideal, since it can save both counterparts in the negotiation a lot of time, money, and aggravation. Our current clients who own car dealerships are proud to tell us that almost 50 percent of their fleet is sold to existing customers who have had a good purchasing experience, in what is obviously a win-win relationship.

But, if the goal is to create mutually beneficial relationships based on trust, why are strategies and tactics important? Doesn't that seem manipulative? First, because not everyone you negotiate with will care about creating a win-win outcome. The "sharks"—or bullies, which you will hear more about in Chapter 8—of this world want to win at all costs and couldn't care less if *you* lose. Second, effective strategies and tactics help generate a number of options to enable both you and your counterpart to accomplish your goals. The more options you have, the more likely it is that you will be able to generate a win-win outcome. Finally, your counterpart will probably use strategies and tactics even if you don't, and the ability to recognize and counter them will enable you to bring the negotiation back to a level playing field. In most situations, strategies and tactics are critical to success. That's why we discuss them in great detail in Part II of this book.

Note that when discussing negotiation, we have chosen to use the word *counterpart* rather than *opponent*. How you view those you negotiate with has a lot to do with your ability to achieve successful outcomes. Looking at those you negotiate with as opponents tends to result in win-lose outcomes. On the other hand, approaching those you negotiate with as counterparts makes you feel a personal obligation to create success for both sides and tends to result in win-win solutions.

Although great negotiators drive a hard bargain, most have the reputation of being both fair and trustworthy. When you have these qualities, people are willing to come back and renegotiate with you at a later date. This book will give you the skills and tools to be a win-win negotiator with a reputation for building effective, long-term relationships in which both counterparts come out winners.

PART I
THE SKILLFUL NEGOTIATOR

"Everybody sells something to somebody every day, whether it's a product, a service, or just a case of making sure that they get their own way."

—*Chris Murray*

1

What Is Negotiation?

"Let us never negotiate out of fear, but never fear to negotiate."

—*John F. Kennedy*

In a research study of university students, the following question was posed to participants: How often do you negotiate—often, seldom, or never? More than 36 percent of the respondents answered "seldom" or "never." Actually, this was a trick question, since the correct answer should have been "always." Everything in life is negotiated, under all conditions, at all times. From asking your significant other to take out the garbage to merging onto the freeway in rush-hour traffic, from determining what time to schedule an appointment with a client to deciding which television program to watch with your family—every aspect of your life is spent in some form of negotiation.

Gerard I. Nierenberg was an American lawyer, author, and expert in negotiation and communication strategy. *Forbes* named Nierenberg "The Father of Negotiation Training" for his exploration of negotiation strategies and tactics as well as his decades of work disseminating the philosophy that "in a successful negotiation, everybody wins." Nierenberg was the author of the first book on the formalized process of negotiation, *The Art of Negotiating*.

He stated, "Whenever people exchange ideas with the intention of changing relationships, whenever they confer for agreement, then they are negotiating."

In short, most of us are involved in negotiations to one degree or another for a good part of any given day. Negotiation should be considered a positive way of structuring the communication process.

Typical Negotiated Transactions

Here is a list of some typical transactions in which you can improve your position by negotiating.

1. Price, terms, and accessory items on an automobile purchase
2. Price, terms, and length of escrow on a home purchase
3. Turnaround time and cost for car or home repairs
4. Which Netflix series your family will watch next
5. How much "free" data is included with your cell phone contract
6. Your salary, vacation time, and job "perks"
7. Scope of work projects and time frame for completion
8. Fees to charge a new client for professional services
9. How much time you allow your children to utilize their electronic devices
10. A date for an event
11. Which parties you will or will not attend during the holiday season
12. A work schedule that is flexible enough to meet your family's needs
13. Merger and acquisition terms
14. What games or apps you will allow your children to download

15. Vacation schedules for employees
16. The time of year you will take your vacation (business) and where you will go (family)
17. What monthly price you'll pay, what speed will be delivered, and how long your Internet provider will lock in the negotiated price
18. The shipping price and delivery date for a product
19. Convincing your significant other to upgrade your widescreen TV from a 42-inch to a 108-inch to truly experience virtual reality
20. Discussing curfew with your teenager

Negotiation Situations

In what other areas in your life or daily routine could you improve your position by negotiating? List them here:

1. _____
   _____
2. _____
   _____
3. _____
   _____
4. _____
   _____
5. _____
   _____

HOW GOOD A NEGOTIATOR ARE YOU?

Like any skill, negotiation can be learned, practiced, and mastered. Personal and professional growth in any area of life usually involves a combination of awareness and risk-taking. We have developed the following assessment to help you determine how good a negotiator you are. The assessment measures the personal characteristics necessary to be a great negotiator. Your answers will help you determine where you have strengths as a negotiator and where you may need improvement.

You can complete the assessment in the book, or complete it online. When you complete the assessment online, we will email you a PDF copy of your results. To complete the assessment online, please go to http://www.peterstark.com/negotiatoreval.

To complete the assessment in the book, circle the number that best reflects where you fall on the scale. The higher the number, the more the characteristic describes you. When you have finished, add up your numbers and put the total in the space provided.

1. I enjoy dealing with other people, and I am committed to building relationships and creating win-win outcomes.

    1   2   3   4   5

2. I have good self-esteem and feel confident opening the negotiation at a high level of aspiration and expectation.

    1   2   3   4   5

3. I work to create a comfortable, professional atmosphere.

    1   2   3   4   5

4. I enjoy coming up with creative solutions to problems.

    1   2   3   4   5

5. I am able to think clearly under pressure.

     1   2   3   4   5

6. I am well prepared prior to entering a negotiation.

     1   2   3   4   5

7. I am able to clearly identify my bottom line in every negotiation. (If I go below or above a certain point, I will walk out.)

     1   2   3   4   5

8. I am willing to ask as many questions as it takes to get the information needed to make the best decision.

     1   2   3   4   5

9. I communicate clearly and concisely.

     1   2   3   4   5

10. I work to see each issue from my counterpart's point of view.

     1   2   3   4   5

11. I confront the issues, not the person.

     1   2   3   4   5

12. I focus on shared interests, not differences.

     1   2   3   4   5

13. I look for ways to "grow the pie"—rather than simply dividing up the existing pieces—thereby expanding the relationship with my counterpart.

    1   2   3   4   5

14. I do not take my counterpart's strategies, tactics, and comments personally.

    1   2   3   4   5

15. I like to uncover the needs, wants, and motivations of counterparts so I can help them achieve their goals.

    1   2   3   4   5

16. I recognize the power of strategies and tactics and use them frequently.

    1   2   3   4   5

17. I know how to effectively counter a counterpart's strategies and tactics.

    1   2   3   4   5

18. When confronted with an aggressive negotiator, I know the tactics that will neutralize the effectiveness of a bully.

    1   2   3   4   5

19. When a counterpart and I come to an agreement on an issue, I ensure that the issue is measurable and time-bound.

    1   2   3   4   5

20. I am a great listener.

1   2   3   4   5

Grand Total: _____

SCORING

90+: You have the characteristics of a great negotiator. You recognize what negotiation requires, and you are willing to apply yourself accordingly. Read on to add new strategies and tactics to your repertoire that will enable you to be even more successful.

80–89: You have the potential to be a skillful negotiator. Reviewing the components of a successful negotiation and learning more about skills, strategies, and tactics will get you well on your way to being even more successful as a negotiator.

65–79: You have a basic understanding of successful negotiation skills. Studying the dynamics of building a relationship and learning the importance of understanding your counterpart's needs will help you make great strides in your negotiations.

20–64: You have taken the all-important first step to becoming a great negotiator by expressing a willingness to learn. Enjoy reading this book. Take your time, and you will begin to understand the principles outlined. Applying these principles will provide you with the tools and skills you need to negotiate with anyone.

2

Negotiation's Four Possible Outcomes

> "The real winners in life are the people who look at every situation with an expectation that they can make it work or make it better."
>
> —*Barbara Pletcher*

A negotiation will end in one of four possible outcomes: lose-lose, win-lose, win-win, or no outcome (no consequences, negative or positive). In most situations, the ideal outcome is win-win.

Lose-Lose

Lose-lose outcomes result when neither party achieves his or her needs or wants. For example, a company requested that our consulting firm provide a proposal for conducting an employee opinion survey. After supplying an estimate, we thought we had the contract, but at the last minute, the client informed us that their company had chosen another consulting firm that had come in with a lower bid. At first it seemed the client had won and we had lost; the client had found a better price for what the company thought would be quality service, and we had lost the opportunity for some new business. Two months later, however, we received a call from the client informing us that our competitor had provided poor service and done an unacceptable job on the project. As a result, the client no longer trusted our competitor. In addition, since the competitor's delays caused the client to miss the opportunity to present the survey results at its all-company meeting, the client also lost.

A second example of a common lose-lose negotiation is a labor strike in which management and labor unions cannot come to a satisfactory agreement. In June 2016, grocery workers across Southern California voted to authorize a strike against the supermarket chains Ralphs and Albertsons, which includes Vons, Pavilions, and Safeway stores. The vote by 47,000 members of United Food and Commercial Workers (UFCW) gave union officials the power to call a strike if the supermarkets didn't concede to the union's demands. In 2003–2004, the UFCW was engaged in a grinding, 141-day walkout, the longest major supermarket strike in US history. During the course of the long walkout, Ralphs and Albertsons lost $1.5 billion in sales, and veteran grocery workers absorbed a 35 percent cut to their pensions to end the strike in 2004. Before the strike, Ralphs, Albertsons, and Vons/Pavilions held almost 60 percent of Southern California's grocery trade, according to the Strategic Resource Group. In 2016, those same stores control about 33 percent.

Almost always in a labor strike, everyone loses. And, as frequently happens in lose-lose negotiations, neither counterpart, if given a choice, would choose to come back to the negotiating table with the same counterpart in the future.

Win-Lose or Lose-Win

The second possible outcome of a negotiation is win-lose or lose-win—when one counterpart wins and the other loses. If you have ever lost a negotiation, you know that the feeling is not pleasant, which leads to one party walking away without meeting his or her needs or wants, unwilling to negotiate with the winner in the future.

A participant in one of our seminars shared a story about how he had obtained a home mortgage loan from a nationwide bank. Almost immediately, the bank had prequalified the borrower, and the terms of the loan had been settled. About thirty-eight days into the loan process, however, the bank informed the borrower that the interest rate was going to change and, in addition, the loan was going to incur additional costs that had not been part of the initial discussion. The borrower's gut feeling was that he should walk out the door and find another lender. But the escrow on the home sale was just forty-five days, and there was not enough time. If the borrower wanted the sale to close on time, he had no choice but to accept the new terms. In this case, the borrower felt he had received less than favorable terms—and lost the negotiation.

You might think that a win-lose outcome is just fine as long as you are the one who comes out the winner, but keep in mind that when you create a win-lose situation, the loser, if given the choice, will most likely refuse to negotiate with you again. (Sometimes, a loser who has no choice may have to negotiate with the same counterpart again, in which case he or she goes into the negotiation bracing for the worst.)

At a negotiation course at San Diego State University, one of our students continually created win-lose outcomes, with himself in the winner's circle. By the final week of the course, not one person in the class would negotiate with him! Creating win-lose outcomes is simply not good business.

It is important to note that almost all win-lose relationships end up lose-lose over time. You can probably remember a time when someone provided you with an unsatisfactory product or service and refused to correct the problem. When you were unable to get your problem resolved, you probably decided you would never do business with that person or company again. In the first round of the negotiation, you lost. But every time you have the opportunity to buy the same product or service again and choose to take your business somewhere else, your counterpart loses. As you can see, as a counterpart in a negotiation, you would be wise to create a win-win outcome.

Win-Win

The ideal outcome for almost all negotiations is win-win. The needs and goals of both parties are met, so they both walk away with a positive feeling—and a willingness to negotiate with each other again. In the negotiation workshops we present, it is rewarding to see the excitement on participants' faces when they realize they have created a win-win outcome.

On July 15, 2015, President Barack Obama accomplished something that every president in the fifty-four years before him had tried unsuccessfully to achieve. Obama and Raul Castro, the brother of the aging former president Fidel Castro, agreed to resume normalized relations between the United States and Cuba.

The United States embargo goes back to the Cold War. In the late 1950s, Fidel Castro led a communist revolution in Cuba, creating tension in the relationship between the United States and Cuba, and between their citizens.

For more than eighteen months, President Obama, along with his team of negotiators, worked secretly to restore normalized relations with Cuba. Some of the significant deal points included:

PRISONER EXCHANGE

Cuba agreed to release Alan Gross, an American who had been jailed since December 2009 for setting up satellite communication networks without the permit required by Cuban law. Cuba also agreed to release CIA spy Rolando Trujillo and fifty political prisoners.

In exchange, the United States agreed to release the last three members of the "Cuban Five," held in prison for sixteen years after they were caught infiltrating anti-Castro Cuban American groups.

TRADE RELATIONS

Obama agreed to loosen restrictions on travel and trade (yes, you can now take up to one hundred dollars' worth of Cuban cigars back home to the States). The United States also agreed to authorize telecommunication companies to bring Internet services to Cuba.

HUMANITARIAN RELATIONS

Cuba agreed to engage with the International Red Cross and United States on human rights and prison conditions.

DIPLOMATIC RELATIONS

On July 20, 2015, Cuba's foreign minister, Bruno Rodriguez, flew to Washington and raised the Cuban flag over its former embassy. On August 14, Secretary of State John Kerry traveled to Havana to reopen the American Embassy, which was built in 1953.

DIVINE INTERVENTION

Even Pope Francis was called into action to deliver personal messages of encouragement to both President Obama and Raul Castro to get this deal done.

WHAT brought this win-win deal to fruition? President Obama's goal, sheer determination, and desire to do what no president was able to do before him. Who won? After years and years of failed negotiations, both countries were granted release of their prisoners. Americans and Cuban Americans are free to travel to Cuba. The Cubans will significantly benefit from the travel and trade revenue that is brought to their country from the United States. Although a minority of far-right Republicans do not feel that Obama obtained enough concessions from Cuba for the United States (they wanted Cuba to restore democracy and make larger commitments for human rights), most people in both countries feel that Castro and Obama broke down steel walls that each country had been staring at, with little or no progress, for more than fifty years.

No Outcome

The fourth possible outcome is no-outcome. Neither party wins or loses. Consider the example of a woman who owns a large commercial piece of real estate and hears that the city government is considering rezoning the area where the property is located. Fearing that the rezoning will lower the value of her property, the owner decides to sell and calls a real estate agent. Once the two people meet, the real estate agent, who is a member of the

zoning commission, tells the property owner that her information is erroneous and there is no plan to rezone the area. The
property owner changes her mind about selling. This particular
negotiation had neither a positive nor a negative outcome.

A second great example where "no outcome" is a real possibility is in buying a car. If you cannot come to terms with the
dealer that are agreeable (win-win) to you, the best thing to do is
walk out. As you walk out, remember this: you will find another
dealer to buy your car from and, most likely, will create a win-win
outcome for yourself. The dealer will end up selling the car you
were negotiating on to another customer, and most likely create a
win-win.

Some people would describe the "no outcome" as either a win-
win outcome or a lose-lose outcome. In the win-win scenario, the
buyer goes and finds the same car with a more favorable price
from another car dealer. The car dealer sells the same car to a
new buyer at a higher price. They both win. In the lose-lose scenario, the car dealer lost a valuable customer. The buyer wasted
his or her time in having to find another car dealership and starting the negotiation process all over. If both parties are willing to
come back to the table and renegotiate with each other at a later
time, then there is no outcome.

The real significance of this no outcome is feeling the need
to stay at the bargaining table and negotiate, even when you are
confident the outcome is not going to be a win-win. Many negotiators think, "If I can gain one or two more deal points, then I
will feel like I have come closer to winning." In some situations
this may be true. In other situations, it would clearly be in your
best interest to get up and walk away. When you think about "no
outcome" rather than winners and losers, it is much easier to get
up and walk away from the negotiation—knowing the next relationships will most likely have a different outcome.

Three Keys to Creating a Win-Win Outcome

In most negotiations, fostering a cooperative atmosphere increases the chances of a win-win outcome. When each party obtains something of greater value in exchange for something on which he or she places a lower value, both parties win. Each of them may have wished for more, but at least they are both satisfied and will be willing to negotiate again later.

Some negotiators have a strong reputation for consistently achieving win-win outcomes in their negotiations. To achieve this favorable reputation for yourself, keep the following guidelines in mind.

1. **Avoid narrowing the negotiation down to one issue.** Focusing on just one issue sets the scene for a win-lose outcome. The most common example is arguing over the price of a product or service. To avoid getting stuck on one issue such as price, try to visualize a juggler. A juggler does not juggle just one ball. In fact, the best jugglers are those who juggle several difficult objects—like knives. Keep this picture in mind when you negotiate: Let's say you want to buy 100 midrange, pro-level tablets for your corporation and your budget is $1,000 per tablet. The model you prefer is listed for $1,299 per tablet. You may be tempted to lock on to the price issue and do your best to get the tablets discounted to $1,000. Why? Because price is the easiest and most logical deal point to discuss. If you take this tack, you may be successful at reducing the price, but you take the chance of laying the foundation for a lose-lose outcome. Keeping that juggler in mind, a better strategy would be to bring up additional deal points to negotiate, such as delivery date, financing, upgrades,

warranty, training, and support—all of which contribute to the overall "price" of the product. Bringing multiple issues to the table provides the opportunity for you to "juggle" the deal points to create a win-win outcome.

2. **Realize that your counterpart does not have the same needs and wants you do.** If you do not take this factor into consideration, you negotiate with the idea that your gain is your counterpart's loss, and vice versa. With that attitude, it is virtually impossible to create a win-win outcome. In the computer example above, most negotiators would assume that the number-one goal of each counterpart would be to get the best respective price. But if price were the most important factor for all buyers, they would all purchase the cheapest computer, and no other model would ever be sold! The reason there are so many models is that buyers almost always have needs other than price that drive the outcome in negotiations.

3. **Do not assume you know your counterpart's needs.** It's very common for negotiators to assume they know exactly what their counterpart wants. For example, a salesperson "knows" that the buyer wants to buy the product or service at the lowest possible price. That may be true—but the buyer may have a much more powerful need that influences his or her decision to buy. By asking probing questions, the salesperson may discover other relevant facts, for example, that the buyer's biggest concern is what his or her boss will think about the wisdom of the purchase decision.

The Importance of Implicit and Explicit Needs in Negotiation

Each counterpart in a negotiation usually has both implicit and explicit needs. Generally, explicit needs involve the product or service (e.g., price, delivery date, terms, warranty, service agreements, training, support, and upgrades). Implicit needs involve the negotiator personally, and include such things as reputation and credibility as a good decision maker, a feeling of being "right" or being liked, a sense of importance, trust in the relationship, loyalty to a company or its product or service, approval of the boss or a significant other, a sense of safety and security, and the ability to act autonomously.

A counterpart will often verbalize his or her explicit needs, but not his or her implicit needs. This is important because implicit needs frequently drive the outcome of a negotiation. The greatest example of this concept is the salesperson who says, "I don't get it. We had the lowest price and a better product, and the customer still went with someone else." Is it possible that trust in the salesperson or the salesperson's product, service, or company may have been the determinant of this negotiation? Most likely yes. Or, is it possible that the salesperson and the buyers were friends or had a long-term business relationship? Once again, quite possibly, yes. Other examples of a negotiator overlooking a counterpart's implicit needs: a baseball team that attempts to negotiate a contract with a player, looking at salary only, without taking into consideration the player's desire to live in a specific city or get more play time; or a company that seeks to hire a high-powered executive away from a competitor by offering increased pay, without realizing that what the executive really values is family time, and that the negotiation would have far more likelihood of success if the company expressed a willingness to discuss flex-time or telecommuting opportunities.

Most novice negotiators acknowledge that their counterparts may have needs that are not immediately apparent. But once an actual negotiation begins, this acknowledgment is forgotten! What is important to note is that, in a negotiation, it is almost always the implicit needs, not the explicit needs, that drive the final decisions to move ahead and proceed to a win-win outcome. It has been our experience that people who believe they are really smart don't make the best negotiators. They aren't good listeners, don't ask questions, and lack the ability to put themselves in their counterpart's shoes. People who think they are smart tend to assume they know what their counterpart wants and believe they have the best and only solution. Remember, to better understand the implicit needs of your counterpart in a negotiation—and have a better chance of bringing the negotiation to a win-win conclusion—you need to ask questions and listen carefully to the responses.

3

The Three Critical Elements: Time, Information, and Power

> "He who knows only his own side of the case,
> knows little of that."
>
> —*John Stuart Mill*

The three most critical elements in negotiation are time (the period over which the negotiation takes place), information (the more you have, the better), and power (which comes in many forms).

Time

Most people consider negotiation an event that has a definite beginning and end. Furthermore, most people think negotiation begins and ends with the actual interactive process between the two parties. Nothing could be further from the truth.

One of our seminar participants sought advice on what strategy to use to ask for a raise during her annual review with her boss. All the options she had considered up to that point had dealt with the face-to-face review session. She had not considered any of the preplanning and information gathering she needed to do to create a powerful negotiation. She had not taken into account such things as documenting her accomplishments over the previous year; researching her boss's goals and figuring out what she could do to help him achieve those goals; exploring the types and amounts of raises her boss had given in the past; and forming a clear vision of her own goals for the negotiation. What this seminar participant did not realize was that the negotiation for the raise began the day she started working for the company and would continue until she started working for someone else. Most negotiations, like life, are a continuous process.

Although many people do not think about it, time and effort should be considered a direct cost associated with negotiation. Too often, negotiators pay a high price for failing to realize this. Ronald Coase, Nobel Prize winner for his work in economics, pointed out that the value of any agreement is reduced by the amount of time and effort that was invested in reaching that agreement. In our seminars, we offer this scenario as a fun example: You are at a car dealership and you think you can get $500 off the price of the car you are negotiating for. How long are you willing to stay at the dealership to achieve your goal? The longer you are willing to stay, the better your chances are of gaining the deal point. When one participant suggests a time limit of, say, five hours, another participant is always quick to point out, "Yes, but how much is your time worth?"

Time plays a critical role in negotiations. Most often, negotiations will conclude in the final 20 percent of the time allowed. This aspect of negotiation follows an interesting rule that seems to apply to life in general. It's called the 80/20 rule, or Pareto's law (after Vilfredo Pareto, the Italian economist and sociologist who defined it). Pareto's law states, "Twenty percent of what you do produces 80 percent of the results; conversely, 80 percent of what you do produces only 20 percent of the results."

In negotiation, this means that 80 percent of your results are generally agreed upon in the last 20 percent of your time. We consistently see this phenomenon in the seminars we present. As the participants negotiate with one another, the seminar leader periodically tells them how much time they have left. Normally, the majority of the negotiations are concluded in the final two minutes.

Time and deadlines can favor either counterpart in a negotiation, depending on the circumstances. Here are a few suggestions that will help you bring time to your side of the table.

1. **Have patience.** Since most concessions and settlements occur in the last 20 percent of the available time, remain levelheaded, and wait for the right moment to act. As a general rule, patience pays.

2. **Be persistent.** Your counterpart is most likely not going to concede to your needs and desires in the beginning of the negotiation. If your first request does not work, try a different strategy, or provide additional information that might persuade your counterpart to make a concession. Don't give up on your first try. Patience and persistence pay off in negotiations.

3. **Move quickly when possible.** There will be times when one or both parties will benefit if negotiations are resolved quickly. If this is the case, sell your counterpart on the benefits to him of a speedy resolution.

4. **Realize deadlines can be moved, changed, or eliminated.** As your deadline comes near, do not panic. You can change it! Have you ever wondered why so many people

run to the post office to file their taxes at the last minute on April 15 when they could easily file an extension, gaining another four months or more to send in their forms?

5. **Know your counterpart's timeline.** In most negotiations, you are better off if you know your counterpart's deadline and she does not know yours. As you near her deadline, your counterpart's stress level will increase, and she will be more likely to make concessions.

6. **Make time work for you.** As a rule, you will not achieve the best outcome quickly. Although there are some exceptions, you will usually be better off moving slowly and with perseverance, even if it means changing your deadline.

Information

When we asked one of our clients how his company had prepared for an upcoming contract claims dispute, he responded, "We have not prepared at all. We are going into the first meeting to check out the vendor's position." The client knew his company owed the vendor some money in cost overruns, but he had done no research to determine how much money was an appropriate amount to pay.

Whenever you know less about the topic being negotiated than your counterpart knows, you are at risk. The side with the most and best information usually receives the better outcome in a negotiation. Why, then, do people fail to get adequate information prior to a negotiation? Because, as we mentioned earlier, most people tend to perceive the negotiation as the actual interaction between the two parties. People seldom think about the information they need until they meet their counterpart face-to-face.

A negotiation is not an event, it is a *process*. It starts long before the face-to-face encounter. In fact, during the actual negotiation, your counterpart is likely to conceal his true interests, needs, and motivations, so your chances of uncovering information at that time are relatively remote. That's why you have to start searching for this information long before you meet. The earlier you start, the easier it is, since people are more willing to give out information prior to starting any formal interaction. For example, before we bought a car, we went to several dealerships and asked questions about the models we were interested in, the financing plans available, and the willingness of individual dealers to negotiate.

Where do you get the information? From anyone or anything with the facts and statistics you need. Browse the Internet; seek multiple bids; talk to your counterpart or to someone who has negotiated with your counterpart in the past; speak with friends, relatives, and others who have been in similar negotiations. The more information you have, the better you will be able to negotiate.

Power

The word *power* has had a bad connotation for many years. It received this reputation because most people associate the word with one side dominating the other. We define power as the ability to influence people or situations. With this definition, power is neither good nor bad. It is the abuse of power that is bad.

TYPES OF POWER

Several types of power *can* influence the outcome of a negotiation. We emphasize the word *can,* because if you have power but don't use it, the power adds no value to the negotiation.

1. **Position.** Some measure of power is conferred based on one's formal position in an organization. For example, a marketing manager can influence the decisions that affect the marketing department. However, the marketing manager has little power to influence the decisions that affect the finance department.

2. **Knowledge or expertise.** People who have knowledge or expertise can wield tremendous power. Of course, knowledge in itself is not powerful. It is the use and application of knowledge and expertise that confers power. Thus, you could be an incredibly bright person and still be powerless.

3. **Character or ethics.** The more trustworthy individuals are, the more power they have in negotiations. The big issue here is whether they do what they say they are going to do—even when they no longer feel like doing it.

4. **Rewards.** People who are able to bestow rewards or perceived rewards hold power. Supervisors, with their ability to give raises, hold power over employees. Money can have power. But money, like anything else, holds very little power if it is not distributed.

5. **Punishment.** Those who have the ability to create a negative outcome for a counterpart have the power of punishment. Managers who have the authority to reprimand and fire employees hold this type of power. State troopers and highway patrol officers, who have the ability to give out speeding tickets, also have this power.

6. **Gender.** Dealing with someone of the opposite sex can confer power. We have recorded many negotiation case studies

in which the turning point came when a woman casually touched a man's hand or arm to make her point, or a man complimented a woman on what she was wearing before starting the negotiation.

7. **Powerlessness.** In some instances, giving up all power can be very powerful. If a kidnapper threatens a hostage with death enough times, the hostage may just challenge the kidnapper to go ahead and kill him. At the point that the hostage gives up power, or control over his own death, the kidnapper actually loses power.

8. **Charisma or personal power.** When we ask participants in our seminars for examples of leaders who have had charisma or personal power, invariably the names of Saint Teresa, John F. Kennedy, Martin Luther King Jr., Ronald Reagan, and Bill Clinton come up. When we ask, "What do all of these leaders have in common?" participants usually respond, "Passion and confidence in what they believe in."

9. **Lack of interest or desire.** In negotiations, as in many other areas of life, the side with the least interest in what is being negotiated holds the most power. If you are buying a house and you really do not care if you purchase the house you are currently negotiating for or the one down the street, you will most likely hold more power in the negotiation—unless, of course, the sellers couldn't care less if they sell the house today or live in it for another ten years!

10. **Craziness.** This may sound funny, but bizarre or irrational behavior can confer a tremendous amount of power. Every organization has someone who blows up or behaves irrationally when confronted with problems. Those who have been

exposed to this type of behavior tend to avoid such individuals. As a result, these individuals are not given many tasks to accomplish because others are afraid to ask them.

Most people have more power than they think. We believe there is a link between a person's self-esteem and the amount of power that person believes he or she has. It has been demonstrated that people with high self-esteem feel they have more viable options—and thus more power to act—in negotiations. The reverse is also true: people with low self-esteem feel powerless. People who feel powerless become apathetic, which means they do not stand a fair chance when they enter a negotiation.

So how do you gain self-esteem? Thorough preparation. The better prepared you are when you walk into a negotiation, the more self-esteem you will have, and the more confident you will be that you can create a win-win outcome.

Rules of Power

When entering a negotiation, remember the following five rules:

1. **Seldom does one side have all the power.** What is encouraging about this point is that, in many negotiations, you may feel that your counterpart has more power than you do. We find that even when we work with incredibly large, well-known Fortune 500 companies that negotiate with one another, one counterpart always feels less powerful than the other. The truth is, the power in a negotiation is usually fairly evenly distributed. Even when you go to a bank asking for a business loan, you, the entrepreneur or customer, still have power: the power to decide which bank you will apply to;

the power to decide what interest rate you will pay; and the power to decide whether you will put up your home as collateral.

It is important to understand how much power you and your counterpart bring to the relationship. Some negotiators try a powerful tactic when they tell their counterpart, "I do not even need you or what you have to offer. I can do business or complete this transaction with another counterpart." This is a tough, sharklike maneuver that makes inexperienced negotiators feel powerless. If a counterpart approaches you with this attitude, ask the following question: "If you do not need me or the products or services I am offering, why did you even agree to meet with me?" Although this sounds like a tough question, it is appropriate to ask. There is a reason your counterpart agreed to meet. Maybe your competitors do not have a good reputation. Maybe they cannot match your price, or maybe their product or service does not have the brand loyalty your product or service has. Or perhaps your competitors cannot deliver the product or service when your counterpart needs it. Asking powerful questions is the only way to uncover just how much power you really have.

2. **Power may be real or apparent.** When I was an instructor at San Diego State University, I knew that cheating was a problem, but I had never made a focused effort to stop the offenders. I figured I would use multiple tests on the final to prevent cheating. Unfortunately, when the term was ending, I didn't have time to scramble the finals, so I had to resort to Plan B. As I was passing out the tests, I announced that I would uphold the university's "policy" on cheating. One bold student asked what that policy was. My response was simple: "If you need to ask, you don't want to know." This was the

first time I had ever seen all sixty students staring at their own paper. Does the university have a policy on cheating? I don't know. But in this situation, whether the power was real or apparent didn't matter. The students *perceived* that I had the power.

3. **Power exists only to the point at which it is accepted.** When we were at the airport on a return trip from Europe, we noted that all the ticketing agents for economy class had at least a twenty-minute line for checking baggage. Yet the business- and first-class agents had not one person in line. Not wanting to wait, we boldly walked up to the business-class agent and got our seat assignments. (We would have gone up to the first-class counter, but we didn't want to push our luck!) Of course, this strategy was successful only because the ticket agent was willing to work with us. But we never would have known if we hadn't tried. In situations like this, we always ask ourselves, "What is the worst thing that could happen?" The worst scenario in this case would have been being sent back to the economy line. No big loss!

4. **Power relationships can change.** Late in the summer of 2014, it was reported that the NFL approached Katy Perry, Rihanna, and Coldplay—their top choices for 2015 halftime show—and asked them for a portion of their postgame tour earnings or some other form of payment in exchange for Super Bowl exposure—and the publicity that usually follows a halftime show.

Many performers would have gladly paid to play at the Super Bowl, but Katy Perry was not one of them. In an Associated Press interview, Perry stated, "Here's where I draw a line in the sand. I want to be invited on my own merits and not with some fine print." When you have a clearly identified bottom line, as Katy Perry did during her Super Bowl performance negotiation, it makes it easy to tell your counterpart what you are willing or unwilling to do. In the end, it was a win-win outcome: the NFL got Katy to play at the Super Bowl, attracting millions of viewers, and Katy received the compensation she believed she deserved.

5. **Power should be tested.** You will never know how much power you have until you test reality. Chances are, you have more power than you think. Remember, power is neither good nor bad. The abuse of power is what is bad.

4

Questioning Skills: How to Uncover Your Counterpart's Needs

"Ignorance is a temporary affliction, remedied
only by asking the right questions."

—Colin Wright

To create a win-win outcome, you need to know your counterpart's needs, wants, and goals. Like a detective, you search for any information that will help you better understand your counterpart's motivations and true intentions. While you are involved in that search process, pay close attention, not only to your counterpart's words, but to his or her actions, reactions, mannerisms, and gestures, as they will offer many clues to your counterpart's thoughts.

Skillful questioning provides you with the maximum amount of information possible for developing your negotiation strategy. Unfortunately, except perhaps in law school, questioning skills are very seldom taught. Remember, the counterpart with the most and best information is the one with the best opportunity to ensure a win-win outcome.

Asking good questions in negotiations can be a challenging proposition. We are reminded of an inexperienced lawyer who was defending a man accused of biting off another man's ear in a brawl. The lawyer asked one of the prosecution's witnesses whether he had actually seen the defendant bite off the man's ear. The witness replied, "No." The lawyer should have quit right there and rested his case. Instead, he went on to ask the witness how he absolutely knew that it was the defendant who had been in the brawl. The witness replied, "Because I saw your client spit out the man's ear." This was the wrong question at the wrong time.

The guidelines in this chapter will help you formulate what questions to ask, how to word them, and when to ask them.

Two Main Types of Questions

There are two main types of questions: closed-ended and restrictive, or open-ended and expansive.

RESTRICTIVE OR CLOSED-ENDED QUESTIONS

Restrictive or closed-ended questions usually seek a specific bit of information, and the answer is often a simple yes or no. But a desire to limit the answer to yes or no is not the only reason to ask a closed question. This type of question can also serve a number of other useful purposes.

First, restrictive questions can be used to direct a conversation to a desired area or gain commitment to a definite position. For example, "If we can meet your needs regarding the price and terms, will you purchase our product today?" Or "Do you want to work on Saturday or Sunday?" Or "You will send the revised quotation to me by Monday, right?"

A second reason to ask closed-ended questions is to break the ice and get a conversation moving forward. For example, as you enter someone's office, you might say, "It certainly is a beautiful day today, isn't it?"

Finally, restrictive questions are helpful when you are trying to gain a deal point or concession from your counterpart. For example, you might ask, "If I am willing to include technical support at no additional charge, would you be willing to pay our full price of $1,400 for each computer?"

The object of restrictive questioning isn't so much to gain a lot of information as to start the conversation, confirm a deal point, or gain a concession from your counterpart.

EXPANSIVE OR OPEN-ENDED QUESTIONS

Generally speaking, open-ended questions yield much more useful information than closed-ended questions. These questions often begin with who, what, where, when, how, or why. Open-ended questions tend to be more informative because they do not lead your counterpart in any specific direction. They are also more productive in revealing your counterpart's objectives, needs, wants, and current situation. Finally, open-ended questions are very effective when you want to uncover your counterpart's behavioral style. Simple yes-or-no answers may not reveal his thoughts or points of view. Expansive questions tend to provide a window into your counterpart's mind.

Here are some typical open-ended questions: "How do you feel about moving out of your home before Christmas?" "You seem to be unhappy with my offer. Which aspects seem to be the biggest problems?" "Why do you feel this model justifies the higher price?" "What type of warranty comes with this product?" "When people have returned this product, what sorts of complaints or problems have they reported?"

Why People Ask Questions

It is in your best interest to ask a lot of questions when negotiating. The following twelve purposes for questioning will help you see why.

1. GAIN INFORMATION

Obtaining information is the most obvious reason for asking questions. You try to fill in gaps where you lack information. When you do not have all the answers, or when you are not sure whether you have the right answers, ask. Don't assume anything when you are negotiating.

Some negotiators believe you should not ask anything of your counterpart unless you already know the answer. We do not subscribe to this philosophy. We often ask questions *because* we do not know the answer! However, there is a time when you should not ask a question to acquire information: if the stakes are really high and negative information could be devastating to your side, don't ask, since you may not be prepared to live with the answer.

For example, if you are trading in an old car to buy a new one and you don't feel the dealer is offering you a fair trade-in value, you might not want to ask, "What does the *Kelley Blue Book* say this car is worth?" if you have not checked the price yourself. (This scenario also highlights the importance of acquiring all the pertinent information prior to entering a negotiation. Once you are at a car lot, the dealer is most likely going to present only the information that is favorable to his position.)

2.CLARIFY OR VERIFY INFORMATION

When your counterpart provides you with information, it is important to clarify and verify that information. Clarifying questions are usually aimed at answering who, what, when, where, why, or how. Questions like "How have you handled the delivery in the past?" or "You will be delivering this product at no charge, won't you?" help clarify and verify deal points that, if not addressed, could leave you at a disadvantage.

3. CHECK UNDERSTANDING AND LEVEL OF INTEREST

How much is your counterpart interested in the outcome of the negotiation? You may want to evaluate his level of commitment to specific deal points, for example, by asking if he would be willing to take a specified amount less than his asking price. Or you may wish to uncover how technically sound your counterpart's knowledge of the topic is. For instance, if you were a mortgage broker and you wanted to check your counterpart's level of understanding, you might ask, "At this LTV [loan-to-value], we will need to include PMI [private mortgage insurance]. Is that going to be a concern for you?" This question addresses both knowledge of the mortgage banking business and the customer's level of commitment to the new deal point.

4. DETERMINE BEHAVIORAL STYLE

What type of person is your counterpart? Where is she coming from? Is she an experienced negotiator? An honest person? Decisive? Thorough? Questions that reveal this kind of information will influence how you negotiate. For example, you might say to your counterpart, "I have a fifty-page document that supports the merit of our position. Would you like to read all fifty pages or would you prefer to look at the two-page summary?" Different people require different strategies. There is a more detailed explanation of behavioral styles in Chapter 9.

5. GAIN PARTICIPATION

Anytime you ask your counterpart a question and let him talk, you gain a twofold benefit: First, your counterpart will like you better. Second, you will learn more about your counterpart than he will learn about you. It is especially important to get your counterpart to talk whenever you've said something he didn't agree with or understand, since letting him talk will have a calming effect. Also, you will be supplied with more information about your counterpart's needs.

One of the most difficult people to negotiate with is the counterpart who sits there, stares at you as you do all the talking, and answers every question with a simple yes or no. With this individual, you will find it in your best interest to talk a lot less and ask more open-ended questions. For example, you might say, "You have not said much about why you are looking at this particular computer software. Why do you feel this model would work best for you and your business?" Or "What features are most important to you?" Or "How do you plan to use the software once it is installed?"

6. GIVE INFORMATION

You may want to give your counterpart information that will help her better understand your needs and goals. For example, you might ask: "Did you know that the *Kelley Blue Book* value of your car is only $8,100?" This type of question can also be used as a test to see whether your counterpart recognizes if your information is correct.

7. START SOMEONE THINKING

Questions that ask for someone's opinion are a great source of information. Asking for people's opinions also tells them you are interested in them and what they have to say. For example, when negotiating the salary for a potential employee, you might ask, "When you think about a great company to work for, what attributes come to mind?" The more you can get your counterpart to talk, the more information you will have for planning your strategy.

8. BRING ATTENTION BACK TO THE SUBJECT

Some counterparts have a tough time getting to the point. Maybe they are intentionally avoiding a sensitive topic. Appropriate questions can help keep the conversation moving along and heading toward your goal.

Salespeople are often taught to find out something personal about a prospect and use this information as a starting point for their presentation. Talking about the personal side is fine, but eventually you will need to change your questioning pattern and get answers for the real reasons you are meeting. This requires asking questions that focus attention back on your desired subject. For example: "Can we get back to the salary issue and benefits package once again? Is it possible to increase the starting salary by five thousand dollars so I can maintain parity with my current benefits package?"

9. REACH AGREEMENT

Questions can serve as a test to determine your counterpart's true aspirations or readiness to confirm agreement. Suppose a seller is asking $250,000 for his house. Because it needs landscaping and a new roof, you ask whether he is willing to take $240,000. The value of this type of question is that the answer lets you know how far apart your goals are from your counterpart's.

10. INCREASE RECEPTION TO YOUR IDEAS

It has been said that people like your ideas a lot better when they feel *they* have come up with those ideas. In other words, giving your counterpart the opportunity to tell you that something needs to be done is a lot better than your saying it needs to be done. For example, we recently had a client call to say a lot of managers in her company were struggling with difficult employees. We asked, "Do you think the managers would benefit from a training session on coaching for improved performance?" We were convinced that this would be beneficial but posed the idea as a question to give the client the opportunity to advocate the training.

11. REDUCE TENSION

Negotiations can become tense. When things go wrong, asking questions that gain further information about your counterpart's viewpoint can be helpful. The added information may enable you to restructure the negotiation. For example, if you are meeting opposition when discussing the idea of mandatory drug testing at a company, you might say, "Every time we talk about mandatory drug testing for all employees, you seem adamantly opposed. Can you share a little about why?"

Another type of question that reduces tension is one that introduces humor into a situation. Recently, a friend was trying to negotiate an extra two days of paid vacation a year. When her boss gave her a blunt no, the room became thick with tension. Her timely response, "Uh-oh, does this mean I should cancel my European tour?" when accompanied by a smile, helped everyone relax.

12. GIVE POSITIVE STROKES OR BUILD RAPPORT

Simply put, a positive strokes question says, "I want to make you feel important." Sometimes you even know the answer and still ask the question. The expression of caring that you give your counterpart is what matters. Suppose your counterpart has received three phone calls from complaining customers and had two employee interruptions during your fifteen-minute meeting. You might ask, "Are you having a tough day?" Or "With all those interruptions, isn't it amazing that you get anything done?"

Keys to Proper Questioning

The way you ask a question is as important as its content. To gain the maximum information about your counterpart's needs and motivations, you have to structure your questions carefully. Following are several key points that will help you gain accurate information.

1. **Have a goal and a questioning plan.** When you are negotiating, it is important to have a goal in mind and a questioning plan that will help you achieve that goal. If you have ever been in a deposition, you know that attorneys are masters at having both a goal and a questioning plan. A lawyer will

walk into the room with a legal pad full of questions that are sequenced in a specific order to ensure that the witness's responses help solidify the lawyer's case.

What type of information will help you make a good decision? How will you go about getting that information? Will you be direct? Will you disguise your questions? Asking direct or closed-ended questions is most helpful when you are trying to confirm a deal point or gain a concession. Open-ended or indirect questions are useful for gaining as much information as possible. For example, when working with a buyer, a direct question like "Do you have the go-ahead to purchase this product in the current budget cycle?" would provide you with a straight yes-or-no answer that would help you with your sales forecast. An indirect question like "Who else needs to be involved in making this type of purchase decision?" would reveal who the real decision makers in the company are.

Having a questioning plan will put you in the action mode and your counterpart in the reaction mode, as he is forced to respond to your questions. With your counterpart reacting, you are in control of the communication process and in a better position to accomplish your negotiation goals.

2. **Know your counterpart.** The more you can find out about your counterpart, the better you can target your questions. For example, some people have a strong need to build a relationship and do not like to address task-related issues before relationship issues have been addressed. Most often, a relationship-oriented person opens every conversation by asking how you are and how your kids are, and maybe discussing the weather or the score in last night's baseball game. The task-oriented person wants to get right down to

the business at hand. If you are a task-oriented person and your counterpart is relationship-oriented, you may give the impression of rudeness if you dive right into the negotiation process without addressing the amenities. On the other hand, if you are a relationship-oriented person and your counterpart is task-oriented, your efforts to initiate a little "small talk" may be seen as wasting precious time. Recognizing and respecting your counterpart's style creates a win-win atmosphere.

What motivates your counterpart? What are her needs and values? How does she approach social interactions? What is her attitude toward time? What categorizes her decision-making process? A greater knowledge of these issues will enable you to make your questions more targeted and specific.

3. **Move from the broad to the narrow.** In the question sequence, it is helpful to start with broad questions. Then, as you gain answers to those, you can refine and hone your questions to eventually yield specific information. For example, "Did you keep maintenance records on your car?" "Yes." "What did you record?" "When I changed the oil and replaced the tires." "How often did you change your oil?" "Every three thousand miles." "What kind of oil did you use?" and so on.

4. **Use proper timing.** We've all experienced situations where we asked the wrong question at the wrong time. It is important to be sensitive to your counterpart's needs and feelings. If your counterpart is not receptive to your question or finds it offensive, two things happen: (1) You do not gain the amount of information you would have with a properly timed question; and (2) your counterpart may become reluctant or even unwilling to negotiate with you in the future. Asking

your husband how his diet is going while he is eating a big dessert is an example of bad timing.

5. **Build on previous responses.** This point is similar to point number 3. As you gain more information, you can make your questions more specific. Negotiators who use this technique are always listening for information they can dive into for more clarification. The more information they have, the better decisions they can make. In the TV series *Columbo*, Peter Falk's character is a master of this technique. "Just one more question," he says. "If you weren't at the murder scene, how did you know the weapon was a knife?"

6. **Ask permission to ask a question.** Asking permission is the polite thing to do. It is also effective because most people will not refuse you if you ask permission. Finally, it starts the swing toward agreement. Once your counterpart has granted you permission, he is more likely to give you a complete answer. Lieutenant Columbo is a master of this technique, too. He constantly returns to the suspect and asks politely, "Can I ask just one more question?"

7. **After you ask a question, stop talking and listen.** Novice negotiators are uncomfortable with silence. Silence is a void, and they feel an overwhelming need to fill it. In fact, some negotiators will even try to answer the question for their counterpart if there is no response. When you ask a question, enjoy the golden silence and give your counterpart ample time to formulate a response.

8. **Take notes.** If you are going to ask questions, we encourage you to take notes. You do not need to take everything down word for word, but capture enough detail to enable you to

re-create the negotiation later, recalling the main points your counterpart made. Taking notes demonstrates that you care about your counterpart's thoughts and are thorough in your investigations, and allows you to recall information as the negotiation proceeds.

A successful negotiator knows the wants, needs, and motivations of his or her counterpart and has a thorough knowledge of the topic of negotiation. The easiest and quickest way to uncover the necessary information is through skillful questioning. With practice, you will find yourself asking better questions and gaining increasingly valuable information.

Designing Purposeful Questions

SCENARIO

You are interviewing for a job as a sales representative for a company that makes software for lawyers. Two of your main goals are to have more flexible working hours and to be able to telecommute a couple of days a week. You might ask the following questions to fulfill various purposes.

Gain Information: "What specific types of experience are you looking for in a sales representative?" (You might not want to ask, "Does the position call for any specific knowledge of the law?" if you are not experienced in that area.)

Clarify or Verify Information: Clarify: "When would you need me to start?" Verify: "This is a full-time position, isn't it?"

Check Understanding and Level of Interest: "What is more important to you—that the salesperson is in the office forty hours a week, or that he increases sales?"

Determine Behavioral Style: "Would you like me to role-play a typical sales presentation? Or would you prefer to see statistics that show how much I increased sales for my last company?"

Gain Participation: "What are your most important goals for your sales team? In what areas are you most hoping to improve sales?"

Give Information: "Did you know that I am fully set up to work from my home office and, in my current position, work two days a week from home?"

Start Someone Thinking: "What attributes do you think are most important in a salesperson?"

Bring Attention Back to the Subject: "Can we get back to the subject of flextime? Does your company require that a person be in the office from nine to five?"

Reach Agreement: "If I could guarantee an increase in your sales volume, would you be willing to consider more flexible working hours?"

Increase Reception to Your Ideas: (If you want to work earlier hours than the typical nine-to-five day and you live on the West Coast): "Don't you think it's best to call on potential customers on the East Coast first thing in the morning?"

Reduce Tension: "Whenever I bring up the subject of flextime, you seem a little uncomfortable. Can you tell me why?"

Give Positive Strokes or Build Rapport: "It's pretty frustrating when you know your product is better than all the others on the market, and yet your sales are not what they should be, isn't it?"

5

Listening Skills: A Powerful Key to Successful Negotiating

"The most important thing in communication is
to hear what isn't being said."

—*Peter Drucker*

Unfortunately, few negotiators know how to be good listeners, and negotiators who are poor listeners miss numerous opportunities to learn more about their counterparts' needs and goals. Statistics indicate that the untrained listener is likely to understand and retain only about 50 percent of a conversation. This relatively poor retention rate drops to an even less impressive 25 percent just forty-eight hours later. This means that an untrained listener's recall of particular conversations will usually be inaccurate and incomplete.

Many communication problems in negotiations can be attributed to poor listening skills. To be a good listener, you must attempt to be objective. Try to understand not just your counterpart's words but the intentions behind his words. Whenever he tells you something, you must ask yourself questions like "Why did he tell me that? What does he think my reaction should be? Was he being honest?" and so on.

The best negotiators are almost always the best listeners. Why does the correlation exist? Invariably, the best negotiators observe the communication skills, both verbal and nonverbal, of their counterparts. They hear and note how other negotiators make effective use of word choice and sentence structure. They realize that when they listen carefully to what their counterpart is saying, they inevitably learn something new.

Experts on listening suggest that we all make at least one major listening mistake each day. For negotiators, such mistakes can be costly. It seems obvious, but studies prove that the most successful negotiators are those who are able to uncover more needs than their less successful colleagues. Effective listening helps negotiators uncover their counterparts' needs and goals, and this information is essential to creating win-win outcomes.

Three Pitfalls in Listening

Negotiators frequently run into three pitfalls that can come between them and effective listening. First, many people believe that negotiating is primarily a job of persuasion, and they think that persuasion means talking. They see talking as an active role and listening as a passive role. What they seem to forget is that persuasion is extremely difficult when you don't know what motivates the people you are trying to persuade!

Second, poor listeners tend to concentrate on what *they* have to say rather than on what their counterpart is saying, and they use their listening time preparing for their next turn to speak. In so doing, they may fail to pay attention to information that could be vital later in the negotiation.

Third, people let their emotional filters or blinders prevent them from hearing what they do not want to hear and seeing what they do not want to see. Words are only a small part of any message. Vocal intonation and nonverbal behavior also play a role.

When a man utters the words "I love you," a wise woman looks beyond those words to his vocal intonation and nonverbal behavior before deciding whether to believe him. (Nonverbal communication will be covered more thoroughly in the next chapter.) Good listeners and observers know how to minimize the effect of their emotional blinders so they can honestly evaluate their counterparts' true feelings.

Attentive Listening Skills

Great listening does not come easily. It is hard work. There are two major types of listening skills: attentive and interactive. The following attentive skills will help you uncover the true messages your counterparts are conveying.

1. **Be motivated to listen.** Knowing that the person with the most information is usually the one in control of a negotiation should give you an incentive to be a better listener. It is wise to set goals for the amount and type of information you hope to receive from your counterpart. The more you can learn, the better off you will be.

2. **If you must speak, ask questions.** To get specific, useful information and uncover your counterpart's needs and goals, you have to continually ask questions. By moving from broad to narrow questions, you will eventually acquire the information you need to make the best decisions.

3. **Be alert to nonverbal cues.** Although it is critical to listen to what your counterpart says, it is equally important to understand the attitudes and motives behind what he says. A

negotiator doesn't usually put his entire message into words. For example, a person's verbal message may convey conviction, while his gestures, facial expressions, and tone of voice convey doubt.

4. **Let your counterpart tell her story first.** Many salespeople have learned the value of this advice the hard way. One printing salesperson told us how he had once tried to impress a new prospect by focusing on his company's specialized work in two- and four-color printing. The prospect responded that it seemed this printing company was probably not the right one for her, since her primary need was for one-color printing. The salesperson replied that, of course, his company did quality one-color work as well, but the prospect had already made up her mind. Had the salesperson let the prospect speak first, he would have been able to tailor his presentation to her needs.

5. **Do not interrupt when your counterpart is speaking.** Interrupting a speaker is not good business. It is rude and, furthermore, may prevent the speaker from revealing information that could be valuable later in the negotiation. Even if your counterpart says something you think is inaccurate, let him finish. You'll find that you can sometimes get the most vital information in a negotiation when your counterpart disagrees with you or shares something that surprises you. If you really listen, rather than interrupting, you will gain valuable insights.

6. **Fight off distractions.** Interruptions and distractions tend to prevent negotiations from proceeding smoothly and may even cause a setback. When you are negotiating, try to create

an environment in which you can think clearly and avoid interruptions. Employees, peers, children, animals, and phones can all distract you and force your eye off the goal.

7. **Do not trust your memory.** Whenever someone tells you something in a negotiation, write it down. It is amazing how much conflicting information can come up later. The ability to refresh your counterpart's memory with facts and figures shared in an earlier session will earn you a tremendous amount of credibility and power. Writing things down may take a few minutes longer, but the results are well worth the time.

8. **Listen with a goal in mind.** If you have a listening goal, you can look for words and nonverbal cues that provide the information you are seeking. When you hear revealing bits of information, such as your counterpart's willingness to concede on the price, you can expand on that information by asking more specific questions.

9. **Look your counterpart in the eye.** Research has shown that, at least in Western culture, a person who looks you in the eye is perceived as trustworthy, honest, and credible. If you want your counterpart to be willing to negotiate with you again in the future, you have to convince her that you have these qualities. So look her in the eye and give her your undivided attention. This will also provide you with an added advantage. Many experienced negotiators have found that with careful attention, they can tell what a counterpart is really thinking and feeling. What message are your counterpart's eyes sending? Is she lying or telling the truth? Is she nervous and desperate to complete the negotiation? Careful attention and observation will help you determine *everything* your

counterpart is saying—verbally and nonverbally. Every once in a while a participant will tell us, "I have had a counterpart look me right in the eye and tell me a boldface lie." It happens. The good news is that when it does happen, most negotiators know how to put safeguards in place for honesty in future negotiations.

10. **React to the message, not the person.** It is helpful to understand *why* your counterpart says the things he says and does the things he does. In a negotiation, the actions people take, and the words they use, reflect their needs and goals. Each counterpart in a negotiation is trying to change the relationship according to his best interests. If your counterpart says or does something you don't understand, ask yourself, would you do the same thing if you were in his shoes? If you find it necessary to react negatively to a counterpart's words or actions, make sure you attack the message, not the person.

11. **Don't get angry.** When you become angry, you turn control over to your counterpart. Anger does not put you in a frame of mind to make the best decisions. Emotions of any kind can hinder your ability to listen effectively. Anger, especially, interferes with the problem-solving processes involved in negotiations; when you are angry, you tend to shut out your counterpart. You might want to use gestures that imply you are angry just to create an effect, but make sure you are really retaining control of your emotions. Remember, if you are ever going to respond with anger, plan it in advance and do it for the impact, not because you lost your cool.

12. **Remember, it is impossible to listen and speak at the same time.** If you are speaking, you are showing your hand and not getting the information you need from your

counterpart. Obviously, you will have to speak at some point so your counterpart can help you meet your goals, but first learn your counterpart's frame of reference. Armed with that information, you will be in control of the negotiation. And when you are in control, you are the one in the driver's seat—you are acting and your counterpart is reacting.

Interactive Listening Skills

Interactive skills ensure that you understand the messages your counterparts are communicating and acknowledge their feelings. Interactive skills include clarifying, verifying, and reflecting.

CLARIFYING

You are *clarifying* when you use facilitative questions to fill in the details, get additional information, and explore all sides of an issue. For example, "What specific information do you need me to provide?" Or, "Precisely when do you want the report?"

VERIFYING

You are *verifying* information when you paraphrase the speaker's words to ensure that you understand her meaning. For example, "As I understand it, your plan is . . ."; "It sounds like you're saying . . ."; or, "This is what you've decided, and the reasons are . . ."

REFLECTING

You are *reflecting* when you make remarks that acknowledge and show empathy for the speaker's feeling. To create win-win outcomes, you must be empathetic. Most of us easily feel empathy for a person who is experiencing something we have experienced ourselves. But true empathy is a skill, not a memory. Negotiators who have developed this skill can be empathetic even with counterparts with whom they have little in common. A negotiator's ability to empathize has been found to significantly affect the counterpart's behavior and attitudes.

To be empathetic, you need to accurately perceive the content of the speaker's message, recognize the emotional components and unexpressed meanings behind the message, and attend to the speaker's feelings. Empathy is not the same thing as sympathy. A *sympathetic* individual adopts another person's feelings as his own; an *empathetic* individual understands and relates to the other person's feelings—while remaining detached. For example, "I can see that you were frustrated because . . ."; "You felt that you didn't get a fair shake because . . ."; or, "You seem very confident that you can do a great job for . . ."

When you are truly practicing reflective listening, you make no judgments, pass along no opinions, and provide no solutions. You simply acknowledge the emotional content of the sender's message. Here are some examples:

Sender:	"How do you expect me to complete the project by next Monday?"
Reflective response:	"It sounds like your workload is overwhelming right now."
Sender:	"Hey, Mary, what's the idea of not approving my requisition for a tablet?
Reflective response:	"I know it's disappointing when requisitions aren't initially approved. Let's talk . . ."

The goal of reflective listening is to acknowledge the emotion your counterpart has conveyed and reflect the content back to your counterpart using *different* words. For example:

Sender:　　　　　　　"I can't believe you want me to do the job in less than a week."

Reflective response:　"Sounds like the deadline is concerning you. Let's talk about our options."

If you properly construct your reflective response, your counterpart's natural reaction will be to provide more explanation and information. You will find the following tips helpful in learning to be empathetic.

1. **Recognize and identify emotions.** Most inexperienced negotiators are not adept at recognizing the myriad emotions. You will find it easier to identify others' emotions if you can easily identify your own. Make it a habit to check how you are feeling. Are you frustrated, stressed, angry, happy, sad, nervous? Then use these skills to identify your counterpart's emotions.

2. **Rephrase the content.** If you restate your counterpart's comments word for word, she will believe you are parroting her. Doing so not only sounds awkward; it also makes your counterpart angry. The key is to restate the content using different words.

3. **Make noncommittal responses.** A good way to start reflective statements is with such phrases as "It sounds like . . ."; "It appears that . . ."; or, "It seems like . . ." These phrases work

well because they are noncommittal. If you blatantly state, "You are angry because . . . ," most people will proceed to tell you why you are incorrect.

4. **Make educated guesses.** Recently, we were involved in a negotiation for the sale of a business. The seller told the potential buyer that the offer he had submitted for buying the business was ridiculous. The buyer responded, "It almost sounds like you are insulted by my offer." The seller replied, "Not insulted, just shocked." Although the buyer was not entirely accurate in his assessment of his counterpart's emotion, it was a good educated guess. Educated guesses work well because if your guess is not entirely accurate, it will most likely create a situation where your counterpart will clarify his true feelings.

A Rule to Remember

If you want to improve your listening skills, consider this: You came into this world with two ears and one mouth—use them in their respective proportions. To succeed in negotiations, you have to understand the needs, wants, and motivations of your counterpart. To understand, you must hear. To hear, you must listen.

6

Nonverbal Behavior:
The Language of Negotiating

"What is going on in the inside shows on the outside."

—*Earl Nightingale*

Research in communication is often misquoted, suggesting that as much as 55 percent of the meaning transmitted between two people in face-to-face communications occurs via general body language, and 38 percent through tone of voice. Following this logic, that would mean that in a negotiation, as little as 7 percent of your message is transmitted through your words. Rationally, we know this cannot be true. When you read an email, which is just words, are you interpreting it using only the 7 percent rationale? Or, can you watch a person speaking a language that you do not speak and understand 93 percent of what is being said? Of course not. While the exact percentages related to nonverbal communication will be debated, it is important to understand the following important facts.

- More than the words, a lot of communication is interpreted through various aspects of nonverbal communication.
- When we feel that we are receiving a mixed message and are unsure about what is being said, we tend to pay closer attention to the nonverbals.

- When trust erodes between negotiation counterparts, tone of voice and body language are harder to control than words.

Communication experts tell us that in a thirty-minute negotiation, two people can send more than 800 different nonverbal messages. If neither participant understands—or is even aware of—these messages, both people are communicating primarily on a subconscious level. No wonder so many negotiations have a negative outcome! Joe Navarro, in his book *What Every BODY Is Saying,* expands on the concept of nonverbal communication signals. In *Nonverbal Selling Power,* Gerhard Gschwandtner discusses the importance of recognizing nonverbal communication signals—in yourself and in your counterpart.

The Three Stages of Nonverbal Negotiation

Learning the art of nonverbal communication is almost as difficult as acquiring fluency in a foreign language. In addition to studying your own gestures and the messages you are conveying to your counterpart, you must also become aware of your counterpart's gestures and their meaning. As you gain experience at recognizing the various aspects of nonverbal communication, you will pass through three distinct stages.

1. **Awareness of Your Counterpart.** After some initial training, you will begin to notice nonverbal signals your counterpart is sending. Is he talking to you with his arms or legs crossed? Is he looking at you eye to eye? Is he covering his mouth while asking a question? You will begin to recognize clusters of signals that may indicate whether your counterpart is honest, trustworthy, bored, angry, or defensive. At first, you will not be 100 percent certain how to handle

these signals, but at least you will be aware that something is going on.

2. **Awareness of Yourself.** Once you begin to realize that your counterpart is telling you things without opening her mouth, it will probably dawn on you that you are also communicating nonverbally. For example, during a negotiation, you may note that your counterpart is sitting back in her chair with both her legs and her arms crossed. Her body language is conveying that she isn't being receptive. Once you are aware of what your counterpart's body language is saying, you may realize that you are also sitting back in your chair, with your notepad on your lap and your legs crossed. To understand your counterpart's body language, you must first be aware of your own.

3. **Using Nonverbal Communication to Manage Yourself and Others.** In the example above, once you become aware of your counterpart's body language, you can change your own nonverbal communication. By putting your notepad on the table, sliding forward in your seat, and uncrossing your legs, you can change your position to a much more receptive one. Once you begin to manage your nonverbal behavior and that of your counterpart, you will start reaping the benefits of "speaking the language." Body language reflects people's true feelings. The better you understand that language, the more you will be able to use it to your advantage.

Gestures Come in Clusters

Skeptics might object that it is difficult to tell what someone is thinking by singling out one gesture. You have probably heard people protest, "I am crossing my arms because I am cold, not because I am being defensive." The skeptics do have a point. A single gesture, like a word taken out of context, is difficult to understand. You cannot be sure of the true meaning of an isolated word or gesture. However, when gestures fit together in clusters, they begin to reveal a more accurate picture of what is going on in your counterpart's mind. For example, a man who is not being totally honest might display a group of congruent gestures, such as refusing to make eye contact, holding his hands around his mouth, touching his face, and fidgeting.

The question usually arises, How accurate are nonverbal communications when compared to verbal ones? After analyzing videotapes of conversations, D. A. Humphries, a British researcher, found that clusters of nonverbal gestures proved to be *more* accurate, truthful representations of the participants' feelings than their words were.

At first, observing and interpreting nonverbal communication may prove difficult. As with any language, you have to study. If you study your own nonverbal behavior and that of others on a daily basis, you will begin to recognize and understand the clustering process. Nonverbal communication is critical to negotiations because it lets you know when you must withdraw or do something different to obtain the outcome you desire.

When scanning a counterpart for clusters of gestures, a good formula to follow is to divide the body into five categories: face and head, body, arms, hands, and legs.

FACE AND HEAD

The face and head truly provide a window into your counterpart's soul. Professional card players are noted for their "poker face," or their ability to hide facial expressions that may tip off other players. Most of your negotiating partners won't have a "poker face," so with just a little practice, you will be able to interpret what their face and head reveal about their inner thoughts. Here are some signs to look for:

- **Broken eye contact:** Someone who is trying to hide something tends to avoid eye contact or break eye contact when speaking less than truthfully.
- **Looking past you:** A counterpart who is bored may gaze past you or glance around the room.
- **Piercing eye contact:** Someone who is angry with you or feels superior may maintain piercing eye contact.
- **Steady eye contact:** Maintaining good eye contact generally indicates that a person is being honest and trustworthy.
- **Head turned slightly:** Someone who is evaluating what you are saying may turn his head slightly to one side, as if wanting to hear you better.
- **Tilted head:** Tilting the head slightly may indicate that your counterpart is uncertain about what is being said.
- **Nodding:** Someone who is in agreement with you usually nods his head as you are speaking.
- **Smiling:** Typically, someone who is confident and in agreement with you smiles at you.

BODY

The body also plays an important role in nonverbal communication. If your counterpart starts to lean closer to you, you will know you are making progress. The more your counterpart likes you and agrees with you, the closer she will be willing to position her body to yours. On the other hand, when you say or do things your counterpart disagrees with or is uncertain about, she will tend to position her body away from you. If your counterpart feels insecure, nervous, or in doubt, she may move from side to side, shifting her weight back and forth.

In addition to being aware of and interpreting your counterpart's body movements, you need to be aware of your own. To send messages that create the likelihood of a win-win outcome, make sure you always position your body toward your counterpart.

Throughout most of the negotiation, your counterpart will most likely maintain consistency in his general body orientation. As you negotiate, watch for subtle shifts or changes in your counterpart's position. These small changes may mean that something is not agreeable to your counterpart, or that he is beginning to lose interest or change his mind. For example, your negotiating partner may sigh, look away, and turn his body slightly to one side. Once you observe the change, it is important to proceed with caution. It might be appropriate to say, "I'm sensing that you may have a concern with the last point we discussed," or it may be time to suggest taking a break.

ARMS

In general, the more open the position of your counterpart's arms, the more receptive she is to the negotiation process. If her arms are folded tightly across her chest, it probably means she is not receptive to your communication. If she moves away from the table and throws her arm over the back of her chair, it may indicate a need for dominance or a negative reaction to something being discussed.

As the negotiation progresses, the arms are one of the best indicators of changes in the nonverbal communication process. For example, when you start the negotiation, your counterpart's arms may be resting openly on the table where you are both sitting. Then, when you mention that your company has a standard deposit of 50 percent on all first-time orders, your counterpart may take her arms off the table and cross them over her chest. That would be a good indication that what you just said was not received well. You may need to clarify your comments or, better yet, ask your counterpart if she has a concern about the 50 percent deposit.

HANDS

There are literally thousands of hand gestures. While hands in isolation don't give you a complete picture of what your counterpart is thinking, they can be very revealing in combination with other aspects of body language. Look for these signs:

- **Open palms:** Open palms are generally considered a positive nonverbal message. This goes back to medieval days when open palms indicated that a person had no weapons. Today they generally indicate that a person has nothing to hide.
- **Hands clasped behind head:** Your counterpart may be signaling a need for dominance or superiority.
- **Steepling of the fingers:** Touching the fingers on one hand to the matching fingers on the opposite hand may be a show of dominance, or may indicate that your counterpart has a need to control the negotiation.
- **Hand wringing:** Generally, wringing the hands is an indicator of apprehension, nervousness, or a lack of confidence.
- **Self-touching gestures:** Involuntary touching gestures to the nose, ear, chin, head, or clothing usually indicate general nervousness and insecurity.

LEGS

If you ask people why they cross their legs, most of them will probably answer that they simply find the position comfortable. Although they think they are being totally honest, they are only partially correct. The position may be comfortable for a while, but if you have ever crossed your legs for a long time, you know that it can eventually become painfully uncomfortable!

Crossing your legs can have a devastating effect on a negotiation. In *How to Read a Person Like a Book,* authors Gerard I. Nierenberg and Henry H. Calero reported on a study of sales transactions. Out of two thousand videotaped transactions, not one sale was made by people who had their legs crossed!

If you want your counterpart to see you as cooperative and trustworthy, do not cross your legs. With your legs uncrossed, feet flat on the floor, and body tilted slightly toward your counterpart, you will have a better chance of sending an open, positive signal.

"Vocabulary" Lesson

When you study a foreign language, you generally take home a list of vocabulary words to learn every night. It's the same with nonverbal communication. If you want to become fluent in the language, you have to do your homework. Study the following list of messages people send through their gestures. Once you have mastered these basics, you will be more skilled at recognizing *all* the messages you and your counterpart in a negotiation are conveying. Then you can use this information to create win-win outcomes.

The Language of Nonverbal Communication

Dominance and Power

Placing feet on desk

Making piercing eye contact

Putting hands behind head or neck

Placing hands on hips

Giving a palm-down
   handshake

Standing while counterpart is
   seated

Steepling (fingertips touching)

Submission and Nervousness

Fidgeting

Making minimum eye contact

Touching hands to face, hair, etc.

Using table to "guard" body

Giving a palm-up handshake

Clearing throat

Disagreement, Anger, and Skepticism

Getting red in the face

Pointing a finger

Squinting

Frowning

Turning body away

Crossing arms or legs

Boredom and Lack of Interest

Failing to make eye contact

Playing with objects on
   desk

Staring blankly

Drumming on table

Picking at clothes

Looking at phone, watch,
   door, etc.

Uncertainty and Indecision

Cleaning glasses

Looking puzzled

Putting fingers to mouth

Biting lip

Pacing back and forth

Tilting head

Suspicion and Dishonesty

Touching nose while speaking

Covering mouth

Avoiding eye contact

Using incongruous gestures

Crossing arms or legs

Moving body away

Evaluation

Nodding

Squinting

Maintaining good eye
   contact

Tilting head slightly

Stroking chin

Touching index finger to lips

Placing hands on chest

Confidence, Cooperation, and Honesty

Leaning forward in seat	Sitting with legs uncrossed
Keeping arms and palms open	Moving with counterpart's
Maintaining great eye contact	rhythm
Placing feet flat on floor	Smiling

Finally, also consider what is generally agreed to be a good context for accurately interpreting nonverbal communication: context, clusters, and congruence.

Context: Where a gesture or other form of nonverbal communication occurs is telling. For example, we most likely behave differently with our boss than with our significant other, or a child. Or a single touch on the shoulder or forearm could have many different meanings, depending on the context.

Clusters: We have identified extensive types of gestures, and given suggestions as to how they could be interpreted. We stress, however, that you would be at a disadvantage in a negotiation if you believe that you're the expert and accurately interpreting the meaning of a single gesture. Crossed arms may simply mean that your counterpart is chilly in the air-conditioning. A person looking beyond you or at the ceiling may mean your counterpart needs more time to think something through, rather than signaling dishonesty or someone who is trying to hide something. Remember, look for several clusters of nonverbals before trying to interpret their meaning.

Congruence: Congruence here means that the nonverbals are in sync with what is being said, or that there is a good fit between the verbal and nonverbal components of the discussion. While not all the particulars may have been agreed to, there is a meaningful relationship between the verbal and nonverbal components of the conversation. Nonverbal demonstrations are more accurate than verbal messages, especially regarding feelings, attitudes, and personally held values.

7

Building Trust in Negotiation

> "To be trusted is a greater compliment than to be loved."
>
> — *George MacDonald*

Making your counterpart trust you is key to successful negotiation. The more confidence your counterpart has in your honesty, integrity, and reliability, the easier you will find it to negotiate a win-win outcome. If, for whatever reason, your counterpart considers you untrustworthy, you will find it difficult to obtain even minor concessions. Think about it. If you were interacting with someone you didn't trust, wouldn't you proceed very cautiously, and compromise very reluctantly, for fear of being victimized?

The 15 Building Blocks of Trust

When it comes to earning someone's trust, actions speak louder than words. Here are fifteen things you can do to build trust with your counterpart.

1. **Demonstrate your competence.** Convincing your counterpart that you have both the expertise and the will to support

your end of the negotiation builds trust. We are all more comfortable with someone we can look to for honest answers, options, and solutions. For example, when you are buying a computer, you have a higher level of trust in a sales associate who gives knowledgeable answers to your questions.

2. **Make sure the nonverbal signals you are sending match the words you are saying.** In Chapter 6, we discussed the fact that your counterpart can tell more about your total message by reading and understanding the nonverbal signals you are sending than by just listening to your words. Congruence between your verbal and nonverbal messages helps create trust in the relationship.

3. **Maintain a professional appearance.** Rightly or wrongly, people do judge a book by its cover. A well-groomed, professional appearance is important. Further enhance your appearance with good posture, a careful choice of words, a clear, confident voice, and calm and open eye contact.

4. **Communicate your good intentions.** Although no counterpart is likely to tolerate repeated mistakes or failures, most people will give greater leeway to an individual if they know his intentions are good. Emphasize that your counterpart's needs and goals are important to you and that you will do whatever it takes to create a lifelong win-win relationship.

5. **Do what you say you are going to do.** In any relationship, you build trust when you keep your promises and honor your commitments. If you tell your counterpart you will discount the price of a product 5 percent, make sure you do so. Each time you fulfill a promise, you let your counterpart know she

can rely on you. Your reliability may be the most important factor in a counterpart's decision to negotiate with you again at a later date. If you do what you say you are going to do—even when the negotiation is over and you may no longer feel like doing it—your counterpart will perceive you as a trusted partner.

6. **Go beyond the conventional relationship.** Recently, we were involved in a contract negotiation. Because we were unfamiliar with the type of contract we were negotiating, we asked our counterpart if we could have more time to study the contract. His response was, "Of course." He then went on to ask us whether we would like samples of some of his competitors' contracts so we could compare them with what he was offering. By providing these contracts to help educate us, he went well beyond the conventional relationship. Our trust in this counterpart went up quickly.

7. **Listen.** Listening openly to your counterpart's ideas, regardless of whether you agree with his position, will provide you with a greater opportunity to build trust. Encourage your counterpart to exchange ideas. Get complete information before expressing your opinion. Also, recognize that your counterpart's opinions and positions might change as the negotiation progresses.

8. **Overcommunicate.** When negotiations get tough, the natural tendency is to communicate less. Resist that tendency! Open, honest communication breeds trust.

9. **Discuss the undiscussables.** Many negotiations or conflicts have issues that are difficult to address. Salary is one example. When people discuss their performance with their

boss, they often find it difficult to bring up the subject of salary. But discussing these types of issues helps build trust and eliminate future problems.

10. **Provide accurate information, without any hidden agenda.** Many negotiators think it is wise to provide their counterparts with as little information as possible. We disagree. To build a win-win relationship, each counterpart has to have enough information to make good decisions that meet both negotiators' goals. We also think it is a good idea to give your counterpart information on both sides of an issue, not just the side you prefer. (Note how the negotiator who supplied us with his competitors' contracts inspired our trust.) Finally, when you do not have all the answers, admit it. To build a lifelong relationship based on trust, you need to communicate accurately and openly.

11. **Be honest—even when it costs you something.** If your counterpart has made a mistake in adding his figures, tell him. A client recently called and told us we had billed him less than we had quoted. This was true, because the client had switched the program we were doing from two half days to one full day, for which we charge less. When we explained this to the client, he replied, "You didn't have to do that. It wasn't that much difference." Our response was, "You didn't have to call us. Maybe that's why we work well together." On the other hand, if *you* make a mistake in your calculations or decision-making, admit it. Doing so goes a long way toward building your credibility.

12. **Be patient.** No one likes to negotiate with the fast-talking salesperson who insists an immediate decision is necessary. Patience breeds trust—and better decisions.

13. **Safeguard for fairness.** It is your responsibility to ensure that your counterpart gets a fair outcome. If the outcome is unfair, will your counterpart be open to negotiating with you again? If you make sure everyone goes away happy, your reputation as a negotiator will take care of itself.

14. **Negotiate for abundance, not scarcity.** When negotiating, most people concentrate on cutting the existing pie into sections and then dividing up those sections. To build trust, focus on creating a bigger pie. As someone once said, "Why waste time fighting over one loaf of bread if you can bake two or three?" If your counterpart in a negotiation wants you to lower the price of your product or service, for example, rather than simply refusing, consider agreeing to lower the price if he will buy more products or extend the length of the service contract.

    An employer set a goal to improve efficiencies and reduce cost by $5 million a year. To engage her employees, she let employees know that 20 percent of the savings achieved each year would be returned in the form of an annual bonus.

15. **Take calculated risks.** One of the fastest ways to build trust in a relationship is to be willing to take calculated risks. For example, if you wanted to purchase a company, you could put a safeguard in place by agreeing to pay $1 million for the company and the existing revenues of $1 million per year. You agree to pay an additional $500,000 for the company if the revenues on both years two and three exceed $1.5 million.

Dealing with the Untrustworthy Counterpart

Building trust in a relationship is a fine idea in theory, you may say, but if you trust everyone you negotiate with, won't some people take advantage of you? Although some individuals do make a living by focusing on short-term goals rather than long-term relationships, these people are in the minority. If you have a choice about negotiating with someone who seems determined to take advantage of you, we encourage you to find someone else to negotiate with. To stay in the relationship just rewards the untrustworthy negotiator.

If you have no choice about negotiating with a counterpart you do not trust, the following five safeguards may prove helpful.

1. **Ensure that every deal point is measurable.** It is important to spell out terms such as customer satisfaction, preferred bidder, high volume, etc.

2. **Ensure that every deal point is time-bound.** When will the installation be completed? If the product or service is ordered, when will the product arrive or when will the service be performed?

3. **Build penalties for nonperformance into the contract.** If the product does not arrive on the date specified, what happens? Is the contract null and void? Will the supplier deduct five hundred dollars off the price for nonperformance?

4. **Build rewards for successful performance into the contract.** If everything goes as planned, what happens? Will the buyer provide the seller with a letter of recommendation?

5. **Agree on a neutral third party to resolve any disputes.** If
there is a dispute, rather than suing each other, will the counterparts agree to mediation or arbitration to resolve it?

The Cycle of Trust

In negotiations, trust is built up or torn down in cycles. If you are
negotiating with a counterpart you do not trust, you will most
likely send signals that indicate your mistrust. If your counterpart recognizes those signals and realizes you do not trust him,
he will probably exhibit self-protective behavior, which will make
you trust him even less. One example of a self-protective behavior is the unwillingness to communicate any information to your
counterpart unless he specifically asks for the information.

If you are negotiating with a counterpart you do trust, your
signals will indicate this, and your counterpart will respond with
open communication and positive actions that will solidify your
trust.

The diagrams on the next page illustrate this concept.

Remember, the benefits of a relationship built on trust far out-
weigh any price you may pay on the rare occasion that you get
burned. With trust, you can build lifelong win-win relationships.

BUILDING TRUST

The negotiator's true belief is
that the people they
are negotiating with can be trusted.

The negotiator observes
the counterpart's positive behaviors
and results. This confirms the negotiator's
belief you can trust people.

The negotiator exhibits
actions that demonstrate
belief and faith in the counterpart.

Through open communication,
positive actions, and results,
the negotiator works hard to gain
and maintain trust of counterpart.

The counterpart observes
negotiator's actions and perceives
that negotiatiator has trust
in the person.

Creates a belief in the
counterpart that you can
trust the person with whom you
are negotiating.

MISTRUST

The negotiator makes negative
assumptions about counterpart and
believes he cannot be trusted.

The negotiator observes the
counterpart's self-protective behaviors
and perceives a lack of trust.

The negotiator exhibits actions
that demonstrate a lack of trust or faith
in the counterpart.

The counterpart
exhibits self-protective
behaviors.

The counterpart observes
negotiator's self-protective behaviors
and perceives a lack of trust.

Reinforces the
counterpart's belief you cannot
trust the negotiator.

Diagrams adapted from *Driving Fear Out of the Workplace* by Kathleen D. Ryan and Daniel K. Oestreich.

8

Sharks, Carp, and Dolphins: Your Negotiating Counterparts

"Act the way you'd like to be and soon you'll be
the way you act."

—*George W. Crane*

When negotiating, you will be dealing with one of three classic types of counterparts: sharks, carp, or dolphins. Each type has a different pattern and style of negotiating and makes different responses to your moves. In *Strategy of the Dolphin,* Dudley Lynch and Paul L. Kordis shed light on how each of these three types of negotiators is likely to respond during a negotiation.

Sharks

When asked, most people will agree they have negotiated with a shark at one time or another. Sharks are the ones with the sharp teeth who are blinded by the notion that there must be a winner and a loser in every negotiation. Sharks believe in scarcity, so they want to get as much as they can in every case, regardless of the cost. They feel they are entitled to do absolutely anything to ensure they don't come out of the negotiation as the loser.

When negotiating, sharks' basic nature is to *take over* or *trade off*. Their primary goal is to beat their counterparts at all costs, but if the sharks' efforts to win are thwarted, they will resort to a more friendly trade-off strategy. Sharks feel comfortable only when they are in total control, and one of their specialties is to force counterparts to play the sharks' game by using crises to cause confusion. A second characteristic of sharks is to assume that they always have the best possible solution to a negotiation. Sharks have a desperate need to be right 100 percent of the time and will go to any extreme to cover up their failures. Because sharks will even lie to hide their shortcomings, you constantly need to be on guard when negotiating with them. One slip and you will be eaten alive!

The overwhelming reason it is so difficult to negotiate with sharks is that they lack the ability to use creative strategies. When their takeover strategy fails, they become even more focused on "the kill." Instead of trying a different strategy, they simply do more of the same, often at a louder, more intense level. Sharks cannot act otherwise, because they are determined to win at all costs, even when going up against the steepest odds.

Sharks are unable or unwilling to try anything different or learn from their mistakes. Their attitude of scarcity dictates their actions and reactions.

If you are a shark, you know that when your style works, it is at the expense of your counterpart, who may feel crippled and resentful. Leaving "kills" in your wake is not in your best long-term professional interest.

Carp

Neither carp nor sharks are well known in negotiating circles as brilliant deal makers. In part, they are blinded by their view of the world. Like sharks, carp believe that they live in a world of scarcity—a world of winners and losers; but unlike sharks, carp believe that they can never be the winners. Because of this belief, they expect that they will never have enough, so they focus their efforts on not losing what they currently have.

When confronted with challenging external events, most of us typically respond with one of the proverbial "three F's": fight, flight, or freeze. Carp typically use only the latter two of these responses. Carp that negotiate with sharks or dolphins will most likely be eaten alive—in fact, carp walk into negotiations expecting to be devoured! Because they have this attitude, they try to avoid making decisions or entering negotiations. They stay in the company of other carp because this is the only environment in which they feel safe.

Since carp do not like any type of confrontation, their normal response is to *give in* or *get out*. Neither of these responses, when used repeatedly, leads to positive outcomes. Carp who repeatedly "get out" by avoiding negotiations find themselves cut off and isolated from everyone except other carp. The "give-in" strategy is even worse. In the worst-case scenario, carp eventually find they have nothing left to give up, so they are eaten alive.

If you are a carp, you need to concentrate on raising your level of aspiration. Research demonstrates that your aspiration level will dictate your outcome. Focus less on preserving what you already have and more on what you can gain through successful negotiation. If you continue to let your past failures dictate your aspiration level, chances are you may even find it difficult to avoid losing what you already have.

Dolphins

In *Strategy of the Dolphin*, Lynch and Kordis chose the dolphin to illustrate the ideal negotiator because of the animal's high intelligence and ability to learn from experience. When dolphins do not get what they want, they quickly and purposefully change their behaviors in pursuit of their goal. For example, dolphins confronted by a shark have the reputation of repeatedly circling the shark and ramming its rib cage, using their bulbous noses as bludgeons. Eventually the shark takes off or sinks helplessly.

As Lynch and Kordis state, "The strategy of the dolphin requires that we think about how we think." In negotiation, dolphins have the ability to successfully adapt to any situation they encounter. If one strategy is unsuccessful, they are quick to learn and respond with a stream of other possibilities.

In the pool of life, sharks are usually successful at eating carp and sometimes even other sharks. But seldom will sharks succeed in eating dolphins. Dolphins are too intelligent and creative not to learn from their mistakes and the mistakes of others.

The major difference among the carp, sharks, and dolphins is that dolphins believe in both potential scarcity and potential abundance. Based on this belief, they learn to leverage what they have and use their resources superbly. Unlike dolphins, sharks and carp tend to view negotiations as a finite experience—they figure their only options are to take over, trade off, give in, or get out. All these outcomes can be considered zero-sum games in which no new wealth is created. The existing wealth is just shifted around. Dolphins are different. They know that over time, all zero-sum strategies tend to degenerate into lose-lose strategies: Sharks run out of victims and trade-offs; carp, using give-in strategies, end up with less and less. It is only the dolphins who believe that successful negotiations can actually create synergy, or more wealth, for both counterparts. This makes dolphins ideal negotiators.

Key Characteristics of Dolphins

Dolphins have four key characteristics:

1. **They plan an infinite rather than a finite game.** Dolphins know that negotiation does not happen in a vacuum—every action they make in a negotiation will have a reaction. They realize that because negotiation, like life, is an infinite game, they may have to deal with their counterpart in the future. This realization increases the likelihood that dolphins will foster cooperation and trust to make the relationship more durable. Finally, instead of cutting up and dividing what already exists (a finite focus), dolphins work with their counterparts to create more than already exists (an infinite focus), an approach that benefits both parties.

2. **They avoid unnecessary conflict by cooperating as long as the other player does likewise.** Dolphins realize that cooperation and trust are critical in any negotiation.

3. **They respond promptly to a "mean" move by retaliating properly.** Dolphins recognize the importance of responding quickly and appropriately when provoked. Putting off a response when you have been dealt an unjust blow invites being misunderstood or victimized. Whether the problem is your teenager testing your home curfew policy or a client altering the terms of a contract, delaying a response sends the

wrong signal, inviting more sharklike behaviors. Dolphins retaliate promptly, when appropriate, to make their needs known and avoid being misunderstood.

4. **While quick to retaliate, they are also quick to forgive.** If a counterpart shows any signs of cooperation, dolphins quickly switch to a more cooperative strategy.

In conclusion, sharks tend to spend the majority of their time trying to control their counterparts and expect to conclude the negotiation with a definite winner and loser. In contrast, dolphins spend the majority of their time building trust and rapport with their counterparts. They do so by discovering their counterparts' true needs and wants. When the needs and wants of both parties are known and there is an atmosphere of trust and cooperation, the possibility of creating a win-win outcome exists. This is the only outcome that produces a net gain in wealth for everyone involved.

The following chart summarizes the differences in thinking among sharks, carp, and dolphins as they negotiate.

Sharks Believe:	Carp Believe:	Dolphins Believe:
They live in a world of scarcity.	They live in a world of scarcity.	They live in a world of potential abundance—negotiations can have infinite outcomes.
It is important to win at all costs.	They must work hard just to maintain what they already have, or minimize their loss.	With cooperation and a focus on viable options, there is potential for each counterpart to end up with more wealth or abundance.

Sharks Believe:	Carp Believe:	Dolphins Believe:
It is vital to focus on the "kill." Victory is all-important.	Confrontation is scary. The only way to deal with conflict is to give in or get out.	When provoked, it is important to react swiftly and purposefully.

Dolphins thrive, not only due to their vision of potential abundance, but also because when challenged, they use strategies and tactics that keep carp and sharks off-balance. Dolphins are quick-thinking, resilient, adaptable, and focused on mutually beneficial outcomes. Like sharks and carp, dolphin negotiators have a desire to win, but they don't have a need for their negotiating partners to lose. They accomplish their goals, but don't burn their counterparts in the process. If you've ever negotiated with a dolphin, chances are you felt positive about the outcome and would be willing to repeat the experience.

9

The Role of Negotiating Styles

> "It is unwise to do unto others as you would have them do unto you. Their tastes may not be the same."
>
> —*George Bernard Shaw*

People often ask us: "What is your model for negotiating?" It is a difficult question to answer because our "model" depends on the person we are negotiating with. For example, a negotiating counterpart who places a high value on building relationships wants to be treated much differently than a counterpart who places a high value on quickly producing results. Some negotiators prefer to handle negotiations face-to-face and have very little need for something in writing, while other negotiators want to see everything in writing and have very little need for face-to-face meetings. A great example of different negotiation styles emerged when a journalist asked the late Golda Meir, prime minister of Israel from 1969 to '74, why she insisted on face-to-face meetings with the Arabs. The journalist commented, "Even divorces are arranged without personal confrontation." Meir aptly replied, "I am not interested in a divorce. I am interested in a marriage."

Successful negotiators cultivate a positive attitude, know their subject matter, and have a firm grasp of the negotiation process.

In addition, they have a good understanding of people. Accomplished negotiators know not only their own personal negotiating style, but also their counterpart's preferred style—and they use this knowledge to build a stronger relationship that will help accomplish their goals.

Understanding Your Counterpart's Negotiating Style

Most people undervalue the impact of behavioral styles on a negotiation. Many negotiators use the same approach in every negotiation and are surprised when they do not get consistent results. But an approach that works well for one counterpart's negotiating style can actually cause deadlock with a counterpart who has a different style.

To better understand the importance of behavioral style, think of the relationships you have with friends, family members, and people at work. Do you treat everyone the same or do you change your approach based on the person with whom you are interacting? Aren't you particularly careful with people who get their feelings hurt easily, and more direct and succinct with people who typically appear focused and rushed for time? With some people, don't you provide a lot of details and facts, while with others you supply just the end results or bottom line?

Everyone is different and every negotiation is different. People who acknowledge these differences and vary their approach to negotiations practice what we call "The Platinum Rule of Negotiation," which is "Do unto others as they want to be done unto." In other words, successful negotiators tailor their approach to the behavioral style and needs of their counterparts.

Each of us tends to approach negotiation with a particular

style or combination of styles, based on our personality, confidence level, self-esteem, and past experiences with negotiation. Understanding the way a person approaches negotiation puts you in a better position to adjust your approach to influence the outcome of the negotiation. Recognizing your counterpart's preferred behavioral style helps you keep your approach within that person's "comfort zone," which leads to the optimal bargaining atmosphere.

Behavioral Style Inventories

There are many different instruments on the market that measure an individual's behavioral or personality style, including the Myers-Briggs Type Indicator, Strength Deployment Inventory, LIFO Communication Survey, Thomas-Kilmann Conflict Mode Instrument, PACE Palette, and StrengthsFinder by Gallup, to name just a few. In our negotiation seminars, we use the Strength Deployment Inventory, published by Personal Strengths Publishing, because we feel it is the only instrument that identifies specific patterns of behavior for two very different areas of life: (1) the behavior people are likely to exhibit when things are going well for them in a relationship and they are feeling in control; and (2) the behavior people are likely to exhibit when they are faced with conflict, stress, and the feeling that things are out of control.

The names of the different behavioral styles vary from one inventory to another, but the characteristics of the various styles are remarkably similar. Most of the instruments present four distinctly different styles. For our purposes, we will identify the styles as the Amiable, the Driver, the Analytical, and the Blend. Each of the four styles has unique characteristics that present different challenges to reaching win-win results in negotiations.

Before we discuss specific, style-related behaviors, let's first consider what behavior is and why people behave so differently. Our behavior is simply a collection of habits that have worked for us in the past. Each of us has a need to be successful and feel good about ourselves, so we make decisions and take actions accordingly. Responses to different social situations, challenges, and conflicts may vary from individual to individual, but while people may use different methods to achieve their ends, their needs are quite similar. Put simply, people need to take actions that will lead to outcomes that make them feel good about themselves.

To gain insight into your own preferred negotiating style, take the ten-question personal inventory on the following pages.

What's Your Behavioral Style as a Negotiator?

Below you will find an assessment that will determine your behavioral style as a negotiator. You can complete the assessment in the book, or complete it online. When you complete the assessment online, we will email you a PDF copy of your results along with additional information on your style as well as negotiating with the other behavioral styles. To complete the assessment online, please go to http://www.peterstark.com/negotiatorstyle.

For each of the following statements listed below, divide ten points among the three possible responses to indicate what is most like you. There is no "right" or "ideal" score. Just remember each row should add up to ten points.

1. **In preparation for a negotiation, you . . .**
    a. ___ Wonder what your counterpart will be like and hope you will not be taken advantage of in the negotiation process.
    b. ___ Mentally prepare to compete with your counterpart, and begin to plan your strategy.

c. ___ Cautiously prepare your case, making sure you have supporting data and research to strengthen your position.

2. **When initially meeting your counterpart, you . . .**
   a. ___ Take time to connect on a personal level and concern yourself with setting a positive tone before beginning the negotiation.
   b. ___ Push to quickly present your goals, facts, and data, having little need for social formalities before getting down to business.
   c. ___ Begin the process slowly, listening to your counterpart's position before presenting your information.

3. **In presenting information during the negotiation, you . . .**
   a. ___ Want to make sure your counterpart knows your concerns, but also knows that you are concerned with his or her position.
   b. ___ Present only information that will strengthen your position.
   c. ___ Have a strong need to present all factual information in a detailed, sequential, and complete manner.

4. **When it is difficult to gain agreement on a point, you are likely to . . .**
   a. ___ Compromise your position if it means you can obtain agreement and preserve the relationship.
   b. ___ Keep pursuing your options until you gain what you want.
   c. ___ Ask questions to further understand your counterpart's position while continuing to present facts to support your position.

5. **When your counterpart surprises you with important information you did not have, you . . .**
   a. ___ Feel that your trust has been violated.

b. ____ Quickly counter assertively with new information of your own.

c. ____ Examine the new information in close detail.

6. **In trying to reach an outcome, at times you . . .**

a. ____ Let the other party determine the outcome for the sake of reaching agreement.

b. ____ Use the other party's weakness to your advantage.

c. ____ Refuse to budge from your position if you feel that you are right and the other party is not being ethical.

7. **During the negotiation, your communication with the other party . . .**

a. ____ Is informal and not always related specifically to the negotiation.

b. ____ Is assertive, direct, and specific to the negotiation.

c. ____ Is cautious, reserved, and unemotional.

8. **When a negotiation is not going well for you, you . . .**

a. ____ Get frustrated and begin to feel you are being personally taken advantage of.

b. ____ Focus on strategies you can use to achieve your desired outcome.

c. ____ Focus on the available facts and data and look for viable alternatives to help you.

9. **When you need additional information from your counterpart, you . . .**

a. ____ Worry that your counterpart will feel pressured or threatened by too many questions.

b. ____ Question your counterpart directly, targeting only specific information you need to be successful.

c. ____ Question your counterpart thoroughly to ensure the facts you have are complete and detailed.

10. At the conclusion of the negotiation, you . . .

   a. ___ Care about what your counterpart thinks about you and try to end the negotiation on a positive note.

   b. ___ Are less concerned about what your counterpart thinks about you and more concerned about whether you have achieved your goals.

   c. ___ Are concerned that your counterpart feels the final outcome was fair.

Column Totals:
   A___Amiable   B___Driver   C___Analytical

Once you have completed the inventory, add the values you assigned for your A responses, B responses, and C responses and record the total in the box provided. To quickly check your math, make sure that the total of all three boxes equals 100 points.

Next, let's interpret what your scores mean. In this inventory, we will refer to the scores in column one as Amiable, column two as Driver, and column three as Analytical.

In many cases, your scores may indicate a clear preference. When people score 50 or above in one style, they are expressing a clear preference for using that style. Another way to interpret your scores is to say that the higher your score is in a particular style, the greater your "comfort zone" is when you are operating in that style.

In some cases, people's scores in the various styles can be fairly close. For purposes of this inventory, if none of your scores is lower than 20 and none is higher than 40, we will note that you do not have a clear preference for any one style, but are comfortable using a variety of styles. Your choice of style may be related to your counterpart's style or influenced by how emotional or committed you are to a particular outcome. This fourth style we will call the "Blend."

People often ask which style is best for negotiating. We emphasize that no one style stands out as superior. Competent, confident negotiators are typically aware of two important factors before going into a negotiation: (1) the style they are personally most confident using; and (2) the style their counterpart most prefers. Experienced negotiators know that people will predictably use the style that is most comfortable for them. They realize that their counterpart's "comfort zone" has developed through a lifetime of interactions with others and learning what works and what doesn't.

Being able to identify a counterpart's preferred style and adapt your own style accordingly can be incredibly helpful in building productive relationships. With that concept in mind, let's take a look at the characteristics that will help you identify your counterpart's preferred style, and consider some tips to building relationships that lead to win-win outcomes.

First, we will discuss Amiables. Negotiators who use the Amiable style have a strong need to feel recognized and valued in the negotiating partnership. In the accompanying chart you will find behavioral characteristics associated with the Amiable style, and discover what you can do to build an effective negotiating partnership with people who use predominantly this style.

Amiables

Behavioral Characteristics	Tips for Building Effective Relationships
Have a strong concern for relationships.	Demonstrate respect and care for the relationship. Be sincere and genuine.
Focus more on feelings, less on facts.	Don't discount personal feelings. Be concerned.

Have a need to be liked.	Recognize the unique contributions or ideas Amiables bring to the table.
Ask many questions and may at times appear unfocused.	Be patient and relaxed. Understand that Amiables may be using questions in an attempt to build rapport with you.
Are trusting.	Negotiate in a manner that builds trust. Understand that Amiables who feel that their trust has been violated will be reluctant to negotiate with you again.
Are typically good listeners.	Ask Amiables for their opinions and feelings about the matter being discussed. Practice being an active listener.
Feel comfortable sharing personal issues and concerns.	Understand that for Amiables, the negotiation is more than just business—it is personal. Never tell Amiables, "Don't take it personally."
Work at a steady pace; don't like to be rushed.	Realize that Amiables may tell you, "Let me think it over and get back to you."
Have a strong desire for harmony.	Remain positive and solution-oriented. Do not go "head-to-head" in a confrontational stance.

Drivers and Amiables are often noted to be at opposite ends of the behavior style continuum. While Amiables are focused on the relationship with their counterpart, Drivers are results-oriented and focused primarily on the bottom line. In the accompanying chart, you will find Driver characteristics and tips for creating an effective negotiating partnership with people who prefer this style.

Drivers

Behavioral Characteristics	Tips for Building Effective Relationships
Have a strong concern for outcomes; consider any relationship with the counterpart as secondary to the outcome or final result.	Know your bottom line. Be prepared. Keep your interactions focused on business. Drivers may perceive you as weak if you discuss personal concerns at the table.
Are focused more on facts, less on feelings.	Do your homework before your initial meeting to raise your confidence level.
Process information quickly; have little need for explanation or detail.	Be direct, focused, and succinct.
Are impatient.	You can "tell" Drivers, but you can't tell them much! Don't try. Ask questions that allow Drivers to discover solutions and suggest acceptable alternatives.
May view their negotiating counterparts as adversaries.	Don't take things personally. For Drivers, business is just business.
Have a strong need to win.	Competitiveness makes it difficult for Drivers to concede points. Try to avoid win-lose scenarios as you look for viable alternatives. But don't give Drivers anything without getting something in return.

Are self-confident and assertive. May at times appear domineering and aggressive.	Raise your level of assertiveness to match theirs.

If your negotiating counterpart appears cautious and reserved, he or she may be using the Analytical style. True Analyticals methodically explore all options, leaving no stone unturned in their quest for a fair and economical outcome. Read the accompanying chart for tips on negotiating with Analyticals.

Analyticals

Behavioral Characteristics	Tips for Building Effective Relationships
Have a strong need for timely, accurate, detailed facts and information.	Prepare thoroughly before beginning the negotiation. Make sure the research you conduct is complete and accurate.
Are uncomfortable about bringing personal feelings into the negotiation.	Keep your discussions factual and business-related.
Process information slowly.	Be patient. Repeat information and provide additional information when requested.
Are economical.	Demonstrate ways in which outcomes will be advantageous; for example, show how money, time, or resources will be conserved.
Can be unemotional and difficult to "read."	Do not take your counterparts' aloofness personally. Understand that proceeding cautiously and unemotionally is a characteristic of the style.

Analyticals

Behavioral Characteristics	Tips for Building Effective Relationships
Are logical and organized.	Recognize your counterparts' ability to organize and logically approach the negotiation process. Genuinely valuing this approach helps build respect and rapport.
Are highly principled.	Be honest and ethical. Analyticals who perceive that they have been deceived or cheated will have little patience with their counterparts.
Speak slowly and directly.	Understand that the ability to process systematically and methodically is a strength of the Analytical style. Don't rush.
Are cautious and detail-oriented.	Respect the Analyticals' need for knowing the details before making concessions.
Ask many questions.	Provide "full disclosure" when answering questions. If you do not provide Analyticals with both the pros and cons of all the alternatives, they will perceive you as dishonest.

The last style we will discuss is the Blend. Blends are people who have no clear preference for one style, but use a combination of styles. As mentioned earlier, Blends are people whose scores are no lower than 20 and no higher than 40 in any one column.

Blends

Behavioral Characteristics	Tips for Building Effective Relationships
Are personable and social.	Take time to connect on a personal note before beginning the negotiation.
Tend to be flexible and adaptable.	Make sure deal points are clarified and specific before finalizing the negotiation.
Enjoy humor—may take business a little less seriously than other styles.	Keep things light and humorous.
Are creative and open to change.	Focus on coming up with a number of viable options. Look for new or unique approaches.
Are team players.	Appeal to their sense of commitment to the team's success.

Determining Your Counterpart's Behavioral Style

Before a negotiation, you are not likely to have the benefit of using an inventory to discover your negotiating counterpart's preferred style of interacting with others! So how do you get this information without an inventory? There are three main ways: (1) general observation, (2) listening, and (3) asking questions.

GENERAL OBSERVATION

You will get your first clues about your counterpart's style through general observation. When you walk into your counterpart's office, look around. The types of things that are displayed on the walls or desk can provide insight into what your counterpart feels is important. Are family pictures or company photos displayed, indicating that relationships are important? If so, you may be negotiating with an Amiable or a Blend. Are the walls covered with plaques and certificates noting achievements and displaying a pride in accomplishment? This may indicate that your counterpart is a Driver. Is the office neat and organized, or are stacks of files and papers lying around? The neater and more organized the office is, the greater the likelihood that you are negotiating with an Analytical. It is important to note that you cannot determine your counterpart's style by observation alone, but you can certainly gain some initial insights.

LISTENING

A second tool for helping you identify your counterpart's style is listening. For example, an employee meets with her company's management team and says she would like to retire within one year. The manager who is a Driver asks, "What is the exact date you would like to retire?" Another manager, an Amiable, asks, "Is there anything we can do to create an environment that would make you want to stay longer?" A third manager, who is a Blend, comments, "Another reason to bring the team together for a happy hour!" And a fourth manager, an Analytical, states, "For the next year, we would like you to write down in detail what you do on a daily basis so we will have a step-by-step manual to train your replacement."

ASKING QUESTIONS

A third way to determine your counterpart's behavioral style is by asking questions and listening carefully to the responses.

For example, to determine if your counterpart is a Driver or an Analytical, you could ask, "We have a sixty-page document that supports our position. Would you like me to review the complete document with you, or would you like to see the two-page summary?" An Analytical will almost always want to review the entire document, while a Driver will usually want to see the two-page summary.

Other good questions to help you determine your negotiating counterpart's style might be, "How are you doing today?" or "How was your weekend?" In response, Amiables will typically give a lot of information, much of it personal. In fact, Amiables will often provide far more information than Drivers or Analyticals want to know! Drivers responding to the same type of questions will simply respond, "Fine," and quickly switch the topic to the business at hand.

Applying Your Knowledge of Behavioral Styles

The ability to identify and understand your counterparts' negotiating styles—and adapt your style accordingly—can help you build productive relationships that lead to win-win outcomes. Remembering the Platinum Rule of Negotiating, "Do unto others as they want to be done unto," will serve you well in every negotiation you enter.

10

Preparing to Negotiate

"Spectacular achievement is always preceded by
spectacular preparation."

—*Robert H. Schuller*

Advance preparation is critical for successful negotiation. Each counterpart walks into a negotiation with certain natural advantages. For example, in a typical buyer-seller relationship, the seller has specific information regarding the actual cost of manufacturing the product or providing the service. The buyer, on the other hand, has the opportunity to get competitive bids and information about the strengths and weaknesses of the seller's product or service. The key goal of advance preparation is to maximize the probability of creating a win-win outcome. The more information you have, the more likely it is that you will be successful. The challenge is that busy people tend to cut corners, and it's very tempting to try to save time by eliminating the hard work of preparation. Don't make this mistake! Before going into a negotiation, make sure you have thoroughly researched all the issues and have established a clear set of goals based on the information you have collected.

Preparing from Both Counterparts' Points of View

When negotiating, your competence and level of confidence rise immensely when you can successfully negotiate either side of the deal, so we encourage you to prepare for every negotiation from your counterpart's point of view as well as your own. The Points of View Questionnaire in this chapter will help you with this important step.

Using the Points of View Questionnaire

Answering the following questions will enable you to fill in the appropriate slots on the questionnaire.

Topic: What topic(s) will be discussed in the negotiation? What is your purpose in the negotiation? What is your counterpart's purpose? Are the purposes the same or different?

Vision: What is your vision of the ideal outcome for this negotiation?

Information Sources: Where will you go to find information that will be helpful in preparing you for this negotiation?

- Will you talk with friends or business associates familiar with this type of negotiation?
- Will you research the topic you are negotiating by using books, videos, or YouTube?
- Will you check reliable sources, such as *Consumer Reports,* the *Kelley Blue Book* (for automobiles), or the local Multiple Listing Service (for homes)?
- Will you shop the competition?

- Will you check product reviews online?
- Will you browse the Internet or check online sources for the same product or service?
- Can you find out more about what to expect from your counterpart by talking to someone who has made similar deals with him or her in the past?
- Can you find out how your counterpart is compensated—by salary or commission? (This information will give you insight into your counterpart's level of motivation.)

As you collect your information, take good notes and jot the relevant facts down in the Points of View Questionnaire. You cannot expect to remember everything, and good notes will be invaluable as the negotiation progresses.

Available Facts: What facts are available to you and your counterpart? Do you both know the retail price of the product, or how many competitors sell the same product? Some information may be available to only one party. For example, the seller may be the only one to know how much the product costs to build.

Negotiable Issues: What are the various issues that can be negotiated? Negotiable issues may include price, quality, delivery date, warranty, training, upgrades, color or style, additional purchases, partial or full shipment, shipping charges, etc.

Needs of Negotiators: What are the needs and interests of the individual negotiators? What are the needs and interests of the business, organization, or entity the individual negotiators represent?

Be sure to consider both the explicit and implicit needs, which we learned about in Chapter 2. Explicit needs are easy to identify because a negotiator will most likely verbalize them. For example, your counterpart will probably tell you that he wants a good price, what finance rate he is willing to pay, when he wants the product or service delivered, and the exact quantity that will satisfy his needs.

Implicit needs are not so easily discovered, since negotiators may not be willing to share them. Implicit needs include things like the desire to be liked or loved; to trust and be trusted; to be respected; to be right; to look good in someone else's eyes; to be "better" or have authority; to get a good deal; to feel listened to; to be recognized; to appear intelligent; to win, regardless of how small the deal point; and to have a relationship. It is important to remember that implicit needs, not explicit needs, usually drive the outcome of negotiations.

Individual or Team: Who will be in the negotiations? Will your side negotiate as a team or will you negotiate as an individual? Will your counterpart negotiate as a team or as an individual?

Style of Negotiators: What is the behavioral style of each negotiator? Are you an Amiable, a Driver, an Analytical, or a Blend? What style is your counterpart? When it comes to approaching the negotiation, are you a carp, a shark, or a dolphin? How will your counterpart approach this negotiation? If this is a repeat negotiation, how has your counterpart dealt with you in the past?

Options or Alternatives: What options or alternatives do both counterparts have for creating a win-win outcome? Generally, the more options or alternatives you have available, the easier it is to meet both counterparts' needs.

- Is this a one-time negotiation, or will you have future negotiations with this counterpart?

- Will any laws or government agencies be involved in the negotiation?
- Could a third party, such as a lawyer or mediator, become involved?

Position on Issues: Have you identified your wish (the best possible outcome), level of comfort (the outcome you would feel comfortable achieving), and bottom line (the line in the sand that you are not willing to cross)? You need to identify these for *each* negotiable issue.

Do you know what your counterpart's wish, level of comfort, and bottom line are on each negotiable issue? How do your initial position and your counterpart's initial position compare? What are the similarities? Differences?

Strategy and Tactics: To accomplish your goals, what strategy or tactics will you use? If you are purchasing a used car, you might use the power of competition, mentioning two competitive cars you are considering, to get the seller to lower her aspirations and price. Or you might use facts and statistics to demonstrate that the price you are offering is a reasonable one. (Strategies and tactics are discussed more thoroughly in Chapter 11.)

BATNA: Are you prepared with a BATNA? BATNA stands for **B**est **A**lternative **T**o a **N**egotiated **A**greement. This concept, originally discussed in the 1981 book *Getting to Yes* by William Ury and Roger Fisher, asks you to consider what alternative(s) will be acceptable to you if your negotiation does not succeed. Having a BATNA allows you to satisfy your interests without your counterpart's agreement. The more important the negotiation is to you, the more important it is for you, both psychologically and tactically, to have a BATNA. A real, viable alternative almost always strengthens your position in a negotiation. For example, if a new company offers you a job and proposes a salary that is within 2 percent of the salary you are receiving at your current company, you can feel confident negotiating a higher salary with the new company because you have a BATNA—staying in your current job, which you really enjoy. Your BATNA should be your measuring stick for agreeing, or not agreeing, to a negotiated outcome with your counterpart.

When developing a BATNA, answer these three questions:

1. What can you do to accomplish your goals if you get up and walk away from the negotiation? Sometimes it may be in your best interest to find another negotiating counterpart. For example, if your counterpart's prices are too high, one option is to go elsewhere to get competitive bids. On other occasions, it may be better to have no agreement. For example, you may make a conscious decision to live without a new car, or whatever else you are negotiating for.

2. What can you do to gain your counterpart's cooperation in helping you achieve your goals? If you are leasing an apartment, will the landlord agree to return your security deposit in full if you leave the property in such good condition that it can immediately be rented to another tenant?

3. If the negotiation breaks down, is it possible to enlist the services of a third party, such as a lawyer or mediator? If the union and management representatives in a labor dispute cannot come to an agreement over a new contract, could the services of a mediator be enlisted?

Agenda: Will you create an agenda? Will your counterpart create an agenda?

Location: Where will the negotiation take place? Your location, your counterpart's location, or a neutral third party's location?

Points of View Questionnaire

Your Side	Counterpart's Side
Topic:	Topic:
Vision:	Vision:
Information Sources:	Information Sources:
Available Facts:	Available Facts:
Negotiable Issues:	Negotiable Issues:
Explicit Needs of Negotiator:	Explicit Needs of Negotiator:
Implicit Needs of Negotiator:	Implicit Needs of Negotiator:
Individual or Team:	Individual or Team:
Style of Negotiator:	Style of Negotiator:
Options or Alternatives:	Options or Alternatives:
Position on Issues:	Known Position on Issues:
Strategy and Tactics:	Strategy and Tactics:
BATNA:	BATNA:
Agenda:	Agenda:
Location:	Location:

Pros and Cons of Various Options

As you fill in the questionnaire, you may begin to wonder: Is it better if I negotiate alone or ask others to be on a negotiating "team" with me? Am I better off meeting in my office or my counterpart's office? Who should create the agenda? These are valid questions, and one benefit of using the questionnaire is that it prompts you to ask them. The truth is, most of these choices have advantages and disadvantages.

Team Versus Individual Negotiations

Some people prefer to negotiate alone, whereas others prefer to negotiate as a team. Before making a decision, you should consider the pros and cons of both sides.

INDIVIDUAL NEGOTIATIONS

Negotiating one-on-one has several advantages:

1. When only one person is negotiating for each side, it is easier to build a relationship based on trust. Each person seems to take a personal interest in seeing that both counterparts accomplish their goals.
2. Making decisions is easier and faster when it is not necessary for either counterpart to consult other people.
3. Neither counterpart is likely to have to worry about what other people will think about the outcome.
4. Neither counterpart can direct questions to the other party's weakest team member, or create disagreement among team members.
5. The negotiation process tends to cost less, since only one person's time is taken up for each side—and time is money.

What are the possible disadvantages of negotiating as an individual? A person who acts alone could become overly emotional and make decisions that are not in his or her best interest. Also, one person may not have enough expertise on the topic being negotiated, and could benefit from the expertise of additional team members.

TEAM NEGOTIATIONS

There are times when negotiating as a team is a wise decision. The advantages to this option are:

1. Having more than one team member can provide access to more expertise. Of course, this is only an advantage if each team member truly has something essential to add to the negotiation process.
2. Generally, when more people are thinking about alternative ways to generate win-win outcomes, success is more likely.
3. There is strength in numbers. Presenting a case as a unified group packs considerable power.
4. The focus is less likely to be on one individual's personality.

Negotiating as a team—or with a team—can also have disadvantages. When multiple personalities are part of the picture, there is a chance that one team member may prove to be a distraction rather than a help, or may have an individual goal that is not in alignment with the team's overall goal. If a team has divided goals, the counterpart will most likely sense the division and try to capitalize on it.

Guidelines for Team Negotiations

If you decide to negotiate as a team, the following guidelines will prove helpful:

- Determine what types of expertise are needed to support your side in the negotiations.
- Find people who have the needed expertise; are good, confident communicators; and work well as a team.

- Hold planning meetings prior to the negotiation to agree on team goals, strategies, and tactics.
- Ensure team members will be available to provide their expertise throughout the negotiation.
- Select a lead negotiator or team captain.
- Select a scribe to keep accurate notes during both the planning meeting and the negotiation.
- Assign roles and responsibilities for each team member.
- Practice! Pull together another team of people to represent the counterpart, and then rehearse your negotiation. A dry run can be extremely helpful for raising the confidence level of all team members.

Location

Is it best to negotiate at your location or your counterpart's location? As you may have guessed by now—it depends! Many experienced negotiators will tell you that negotiating at your location is preferable. Being in your "home court" is generally perceived as an advantage for a number of reasons. You are most comfortable in a familiar environment; you have increased access to valuable information and resources; you save on travel time and expenses; and you are able to sit or stand behind your own desk, which communicates power. Of course, you may not always have the luxury of negotiating in your own environment. A buyer, for example, may have to go to a store to negotiate.

Even when you *can* negotiate on your own turf, there may be times when going to your counterpart's location or a neutral third-party location, like a hotel, can be to your advantage. Sometimes you may *not* want access to additional information (like a deposition in a lawsuit) or resources. You may want to have the option of returning to your own office to consider what information to present and how to present it. You may feel it is easier to devote your full time to the negotiation without the distractions or interruptions that may occur in your own office. Or you may want to have time to think about your counterpart's proposal or get more information without your counterpart being present. In this case, it is easier to excuse yourself from your counterpart's location than to ask your counterpart to leave yours.

The bottom line: If you have thoroughly prepared for a negotiation, the location will usually not make much difference.

AGENDA

To optimize the chances of a successful negotiation, you should utilize an agenda. But who should prepare it? An agenda can be created by either counterpart—or both counterparts. If you create the agenda and present it to your counterpart, you have the advantage of setting the topics to be discussed and the order in which they will be considered. Generally, you are better prepared for a negotiation when you have created the agenda yourself.

However, taking the initiative in preparing the agenda can also have drawbacks. First, you reveal your positions to your counterpart in advance, which gives him or her opportunity to prepare counters to your positions. Second, you lose the opportunity to "hear out" your counterpart before presenting your side.

If you prepare the agenda, we recommend two types: a summary agenda that you present to your counterpart to obtain a general agreement to guide the negotiation, and a second agenda that you keep to use during the negotiation to guide your team through all the details. You will find it helpful to create a checklist to ensure that each deal point is covered.

Opening the Negotiation

Some individuals like to open negotiations with a little light conversation, asking unrelated questions like "Did you play golf this weekend?" If you are comfortable with this approach, we recommend it. However, if you are uncomfortable "making conversation," don't force it—get right down to the topic to be negotiated.

Never open negotiations before you are prepared. If someone tries to start negotiating before you feel ready, just be direct. Say, "I am not ready at this time," and reschedule the meeting.

If possible, allow your counterpart to talk first. As long as you have clearly identified your wish, aspiration, and bottom line ahead of time, you don't have to worry about being swayed by an outlandish first offer. Hearing your counterpart's opening remarks gives you the opportunity to change your strategy, tactics, and level of aspiration, if appropriate. If you must talk first, ask questions to ensure you have the maximum amount of information prior to stating your position.

Breaking a Deadlock

No matter how well you prepare, you may sometimes find yourself in a negotiation that has reached a deadlock. Most deadlocks occur because counterparts sense their interests are in competition with each other. When this happens, tensions run high, and counterparts may even be willing to accept a lose-lose outcome, since they feel they will never be able to reach a satisfactory agreement. One problem is that each counterpart is operating under the influence of his or her own perceptions, which may or may not reflect reality. The following suggestions are helpful for breaking a deadlock:

1. **Ask open-ended questions.** When a negotiation is dead-locked, the counterparts tend to do a lot of telling and not much listening. One of the most effective ways to turn the situation around and set a better atmosphere for a successful relationship is to start asking open-ended questions.

2. **Listen actively.** When counterparts are busy telling each other what they want and need, and not doing a very good job of listening to each other's needs, it's difficult for them to find any common ground. Truly listening to your counterpart is the only way to even begin to understand his reality—and convinces your counterpart that you really do care about his needs.

3. **Practice empathy.** Ask yourself, "If I were in my counter-part's shoes, would I be making the same demands or taking the same position that she is?" If the answer is yes, try to figure out how to generate other options that will help accomplish your counterpart's goals while at the same time protecting your interests.

4. **Focus on the issues.** Counterparts who find their negotiation deadlocked often start personalizing their comments rather than sticking to the issues. Reaching a win-win outcome will be a lot more likely if you avoid getting personal and stay focused on the issues, needs, and interest of both counterparts.

5. **Clarify individual and mutual goals.** Try not to get so stuck on preserving and enhancing your own goals and needs

that you can't even see your counterpart's. Perhaps they are not mutually exclusive.

6. **Isolate agreement and gain "yes" momentum.** Start with small deal points that are easy to agree on. Building "yes" momentum should make it easier to reach agreement on the tougher issues.

7. **Generate alternative solutions.** It may be beneficial for one or both counterparts to brainstorm a list of alternative solutions. If each counterpart's most desired option will not work, what are the second-, third-, and fourth-best options?

8. **Take a break.** When tensions are high, counterparts may begin to say things they will regret later. To avoid this, take a break and come back to the bargaining table at another time.

9. **Set a time for getting back together.** If you are going to take a break, setting a specific, mutually agreeable time to reopen the negotiation is important.

10. **Involve a neutral third party.** When counterparts find themselves arguing for different solutions to the same problem, finding alternatives can be difficult. A neutral third party, or mediator, can be very helpful in breaking the deadlock.

Preparing for Success

As we have stated repeatedly, the most successful negotiators are those who are the most prepared. Addressing each section on the Points of View Questionnaire and carefully considering the pros and cons of all the options before every negotiation will help you:

- Set clear goals and strategies.
- Enter the negotiation well armed with facts.
- Think of alternatives for a successful outcome.
- Get a good idea of what to expect from your counterpart—and how to respond to his or her proposals and tactics.

11

Negotiating over Email, Text, or Phone

A lthough many of us feel confident in our negotiation skills when we are meeting face-to-face with our counterparts, some may find it easier to stay objective, strong, and focused on achieving their goals when negotiating by email. One obvious disadvantage when negotiating by email is that you lose the ability to read and interpret your counterpart's vocal intonation and nonverbal behavior (though it is also impossible to notice nonverbal behavior such as body language over the phone). A second disadvantage of email or text negotiations is that they allow for one counterpart to simply drop off and not respond to future emails or texts if the negotiation is not going his way. It is also easier to lie, bluff, or make a declarative, divisive statement when you are not looking your counterpart in the eye. Lastly, it is a lot easier to *say no* over electronic platforms, making it a lot more difficult to brainstorm possible win-win solutions.

Email has been a part of our everyday life now for over twenty years. One of the reasons some people like negotiating by email is that is saves time, especially when multiple people are involved.

Analytical negotiators, especially, tend to avoid high-pressure sales situations, common when purchasing a car or a timeshare, making them more likely to negotiate over email or text.

20 Keys to Succeeding in Electronic Negotiations

We usually recommend meeting face-to-face with your counterpart for the sole purpose of building rapport for successful negotiations. But if you must negotiate over text, email, or phone, here are the keys to creating that win-win outcome:

1. **Know exactly what you want.** Know the features and options that you require before you initiate a negotiation by email or phone. Check the Internet so you know the upsides and downsides of what you are negotiating.

2. **Know that statistics are on your side.** In our experience working with car dealerships and with other frequently purchased big-ticket items, up to 45 percent of the sales are now done over the Internet. That percentage is only going to increase over time.

3. **Do your research.** When buying a new car, for example, check resources such as the *Kelley Blue Book* and Carfax.com to find the most complete and accurate information.

4. **Let the counterpart know that you expect the best price or best possible deal.**

5. **Introduce the power of competition.** Let the counterpart know that you expect the best and fairest deal possible; oth-

erwise you will go to a competitor who can offer that to you. Solicit offers from at least three competitors.

6. **Be ready to buy:** Let the counterpart know that if the deal is right, you are prepared to finalize the deal that day.

7. **Choose your subject lines carefully:** Your email subject line sets the stage for a positive negotiation. "Request for a better price" is going to elicit a different type of negotiation than "Interested in learning more about your XYX Product."

8. **Say no to counterparts that encourage you to meet face-to-face to receive an even better price.** Although we stated initially the importance of meeting face-to-face to build a relationship, once the negotiation is under way and you are negotiating with multiple counterparts, it may be in your best interest to keep the negotiation electronic. Let your counterpart know that you have been offered the same option from competitors and you do not intend to waste your time driving back and forth between competitors to find the very best deal. It is much harder to walk away when you have invested time to drive to your counterpart's location.

9. **Acknowledge emotion or show empathy:** Remember, at the other end of the inbox is a human being. Email and texts make it easy to leave out all emotion. Make an effort to build a relationship. Great negotiators are able to read between the lines and make an educated guess as to what their counterpart is feeling. For example, respond to an angry and frustrated co-worker this way: "Larry, thanks for your email regarding the XYZ project. It sounds like you are frustrated that we have met on this project two times before and the problems are still not resolved. I share the same frustrations."

10. **Demonstrate confidence that you can find a mutually acceptable outcome.** To continue with the previous example, you might add, "I look forward to meeting with you this afternoon, and I am confident we can gain resolution on the issues where we have concerns."

11. **Be willing to walk away.** If the counterpart is not willing to negotiate with you over the phone or online, be willing to walk away. Even for people whose negotiation style is Amiable, and don't like conflict, this one is easy—just don't return their email or call them back.

12. **Be patient:** One of the biggest advantages of negotiating over the Internet is that it gives you time to make the right decision. Don't be too eager to pull the trigger and make a deal. Just as a counterpart can sense your eagerness to come to an agreement in person, the same feelings can be transmitted over the Internet with a stroke of a key. If your counterpart senses you are too eager to make a deal happen, she will use that to her advantage.

13. **Ask for help.** One big advantage of email negotiations versus face-to-face negotiations is that you can easily ask for help using your professional or personal network. Solicit information and guidance from family or friends who are experienced negotiators to gain ideas for strategy and tactics.

14. **Keep track of important emails:** Make sure you refer to deal points mentioned in any previous email chains in order to solidify your negotiation.

15. **Ask more open-ended, clarifying, or option-generating questions.** Our research has shown that when negotiating

by email, people ask fewer questions, and when they do ask questions, they tend to ask closed-ended ones that can be answered with a simple yes or no. Emails should give you the confidence to ask even the questions that you would never ask or would be hesitant to ask in person.

16. **Use strategies and tactics.** Just as you would if you were negotiating face-to-face, utilize the 101 strategies and tactics located in this book to improve your position. As you finalize the two best offers, improve your deal by sharing pieces of one counterpart's deal with a competitor to see they can improve their deal.

17. **Reread your emails.** Since it may be difficult to retract a concession made erroneously, we encourage you not to multitask, but rather to stay focused and reread each email before you hit Send. Also, don't let your emotions get the best of you if your counterpart triggers a negative response. Remember, an email can be shared with your entire network in a single post.

18. **Be willing to switch communication formats.** Knowing when to send an email, when to pick up the phone, or when to go meet in person is the mark of a great negotiator. If your counterpart is not responding to your emails, or responds in a way that makes you believe you are moving further away from your goal, pick up the phone or go talk to him in person.

19. **Bring your documentation:** When you do go to meet your counterpart face-to-face and finalize the deal, bring all your email correspondence and documentation just in case your counterpart tries to back out of an agreement point. This

way you will be well prepared to stand firm on the deal you
agreed to.

20. **Celebrate your success:** By negotiating electronically,
    you have saved time and energy by not having to go meet in
    person, and you have negotiated with several counterparts
    simultaneously to improve your deal. Best of all, you have
    accomplished your goals with the simple touch of the Send
    key—take time to celebrate!

12

Asking for a Pay Raise

10 Steps for Negotiating a Pay Raise

Several times a year, participants will ask us, "Do you have any tips for asking for a raise?" Any negotiation regarding a sensitive issue like salary can be difficult to negotiate. Salary increases can impact departmental budgets or create tension with other employees who feel they are also entitled to a raise, adding to the difficulty of asking for a raise. On a personal level, not getting the raise could ultimately impact your ability to live your preferred lifestyle. If you are going to tackle this challenge, you need a plan. The following ten tips will help you maximize your chances of obtaining a raise.

1. **Build your reputation.** When we use the word *reputation*, it is important to note that there are only two types of reputations: good ones and bad ones. Do you do exactly what is required for your job or do you go above and beyond in your tasks? For example, do you work exactly your scheduled hours or are you willing to put in extra effort when required? Do you volunteer for additional assignments? Do you have

a cheerful attitude when requests are made for your assistance? Do you take the time to solve the tough problems at work? The tougher the problems you are able to solve for your team or organization, the higher your perceived value when you negotiate a raise.

The best opportunity to receive a raise is when your boss feels that the results you produce are significant. To put it another way, when your boss can credit her success to the great work you've produced, that's when you are in a strong position to ask for a raise. When you produce results, your success rate in receiving a raise increases significantly.

2. **Think about timing.** When it comes to asking for a raise, timing is everything. The best time to ask for a raise is when your company is financially strong, it is outperforming the budget, your performance is stellar, and you have a great relationship with your boss.

3. **Know what you are worth.** In asking for a raise, it is critical that you know the value of your worth. Value can be divided into two areas: your intrinsic value to your current company and your extrinsic value (or marketable worth based on your skills and talents) to other potential employers. It is important to understand the difference between your intrinsic and extrinsic value because they could play a large role in deciding what to ask for and what you'll actually receive when asking for a raise. For example, you may be an excellent writer, and if your company does not utilize your writing skills, you will have low intrinsic value. But you could market that skill to another organization in need of it, helping you gain a higher extrinsic value.

The best way to know what you are worth is to search the

current job market. You can find salary information quite easily on sites like Salary.com, PayScale, or Glassdoor. This type of information is critical to your success.

Nothing will give you more credibility and confidence than ensuring your research is 100 percent accurate. And nothing will cause you to lose credibility faster than your boss pointing out there are holes in your research.

4. **Clarify your goals.** In negotiation, what makes up a positive end result varies from person to person. Benefits like shorter commutes, laid-back work cultures, choosing your own job title, robust medical plans and retirement plans, and work-life culture play a key role in how someone will steer a negotiation. You may succeed in negotiating a higher salary, but is the consequence of working later hours, for example, worth it to you? Success is all about the accomplishment of achieving your predetermined goals. Being confident about your personal goals is helpful in knowing what to ask for from your boss.

   Set a monetary goal. Be clear on what you feel is fair and be able to explain in detail why you feel that amount of raise is fair. Decide on the minimum amount you are willing to accept (bottom line), your level of comfort, and your wish (for example, the salary that would cause you to walk out the door and not look back versus the salary that makes you jump for joy).

5. **Prepare for your meeting.** Before you meet with your boss, you must be prepared and feel confident you have earned the right to ask for a raise. It will be helpful to point out things like your three most significant accomplishments at work. It will also be helpful to focus on how you will add significant value in three or four areas that you are responsible for in the

year to come. Don't rely on the fact that you show up to work on time each day—rather focus on significant and specific accomplishments such as the fact that you have exceeded your sales quota by 50 percent or more each quarter.

In preparing for this meeting, you will want to prepare for all possibilities, such as:

- Succeeding in getting the raise you want
- Getting no raise and waiting until your next review
- Being reassigned to a new position with more responsibility that pays more money
- Taking on additional responsibilities
- Looking for a new job if you don't get the raise
- Asking for other benefits instead of a raise, such as a bigger office, a laptop, the ability to work from home, or working part-time instead of full-time
- Not being able to get a raise at the moment, but asking your boss for a timeline as to when that could happen

It will also be helpful to know your boss's needs and goals and demonstrate how your future significant accomplishments will ensure that you and your boss succeed.

6. **Role-play prior to meeting with your boss.** Asking for a raise is no easy task. We encourage you to practice with a friend or relative who can give you critical feedback on your ask. Let the counterpart play the role of your boss. The counterpart should be encouraged to ask the tough questions a boss is likely to ask, and provide objections such as budgetary restraints or that a raise is not possible at this time. Role-play two or three times and you will feel your level of confidence rise with each practice.

7. **Meet with your boss.** When you meet with your boss, have an agenda that follows these basic guidelines:

- Schedule a meeting in advance with your boss so that you walk in confident and prepared, as opposed to frazzled and panicked in an impromptu meeting. Have a transition statement prepared to help bridge the discussion from small talk to "raise" talk. For example, you might say, "I am really grateful for the opportunity to meet with you this afternoon. I want to talk about my past accomplishments, my future contributions to the company, and specifically about my compensation."

- Lead your boss through a five-minute presentation that outlines your past significant accomplishments, your proposed significant future contributions, and your salary survey research. We do not recommend giving your boss the outline of this presentation on paper prior to your meeting, as it could put her on the defensive before having a chance to hear you out. Be aware of positive nonverbal communication. Positive nonverbal communication includes: leaning forward in your chair, maintaining eye contact with your boss, and keeping hands and arms open and legs uncrossed. To get your boss to mirror your positive nonverbal behaviors, you can ask your boss open-ended questions. Remember, your boss will most likely not concede to your raise when she is exhibiting negative nonverbal communication.

- Confirm your deal points in writing. If a raise is agreed to, confirm when the raise will go into effect and how much the raise will be. If a raise is not an option at that time, confirm in writing what conditions and time frames are needed to be eligible for a raise.

- Thank your boss for meeting with you (and, hopefully, for giving you a raise). Bosses do not get enough positive feedback. Take the time to thank him even if the raise is not everything you had hoped for or if you got no raise at all. One of the greatest tests of an employee's character is how he handles success, and even more telling is how he handles rejection or adversity.

8. **Stay objective.** Never resort to an emotional plea, such as complaining that you do not have enough money to pay your mortgage or car payment. Bosses are not responsible for ensuring that you can live within your financial means. You are much better off focusing on your past contributions, future contributions, and what the salary surveys tell you and your boss what you are worth.

9. **Anticipate objections.** Almost every boss is going to provide you with some type of objection when it comes to asking for a raise. This is the time you want to stay objective and once again review what your past significant accomplishments are, what your future significant contributions are going to be, and what your market research states about a fair salary for a person in your position.

Here are some of the most common objections you'll hear from your boss, and some counters to them:

Objection: "Right now, you are the highest-paid person in your job category at our company."

Counter: Switch the focus from what others inside your company are making compared to you, to what others in competitive companies are making compared to you.

Objection: Your boss states that he will not be able to sell his boss on another salary increase, since there have already been many in the company.

Counter: Focus once again on your past significant accomplishments, your future significant contributions, and the research that supports your higher salary.

Objection: "It is not in our budget."

Counter: Focus on the future. Agree with your boss on what you need to do differently to add even more value to the organization and justify a raise. Also gain your boss's commitment on how your future success is going to be measured and within what time frame you will eligible to receive this raise.

Objection: "You are pricing yourself out of the market." Or, "This position does not warrant another increase in salary." This is the boss's way of telling you that you are becoming more expensive than the value your position is adding to the company.

Counter: First, do not take this objection personally. Focus your conversation on what you need to do differently so that you continue to add more value for your boss and the organization.

Objection: "Let's wait until your next performance review." Bosses are great at putting off your raise until some future point in time.

Counter: If your boss is adamant about waiting until some future time, tell your boss that you really need to evaluate your future with the company and you were hoping that something could be done immediately regarding your salary.

Remember, one of the fastest ways to gain a raise, and at the same time effectively counter any objections, is to search for a new job that offers what you are looking for in terms of compensation. Many times, potential employers will put together an attractive package to acquire talent from other companies. If a potential employer asks you what you currently make, or offers you a starting salary that is not a big enough incentive to leave a job you are happy with, a great line to use is, "To leave my current job, my salary requirement is $89,000."

10. **Celebrate your success.** Anytime you get a raise, you should celebrate! Yes, any raise, no matter how small, is a significant personal and professional accomplishment. Go out and do what makes you happy, whether it is dinner and drinks out on the town or a movie night, or maybe a massage. Whatever brings you happiness, a raise is a time worthy of celebrating. Go for it!

13

Negotiating at Garage Sales, Swap Meets, or Local Craft Fairs

One of the first things tourists will do when disembarking a cruise ship at an exotic location is shop at the local markets. It is always interesting to see how many of these tourists bought the exact same merchandise but at different prices. Pay attention to these ten tips for ensuring the best negotiation at garage sales, flea markets, swap meets, craft fairs, or at markets (yes, even at exotic vacation spots!):

1. **Know the lay of the land.** Walk the area first and see what people are buying. Check out if there are multiple vendors selling the same or similar products. Listen in on negotiations with other people to determine the vendor's opening bid and what they actually sell the product for.

2. **Demonstrate low commitment:** Do not communicate, either verbally or nonverbally, that you have already bought the product you desire in your mind. Comments like "Mom would really like this" or "That would look great in our kitchen" will

not be helpful to you in driving a competitive price. As you meet with a vendor, remember there is most likely someone else close by who is willing to sell the same type of product at a lower cost. A great line in these situations is "I would like to buy this . . . but not for that much."

3. **Set a goal, a wish, and a walkaway bottom line.** As you look at the item you are interested in, think about what you'd be willing to pay for it. Let's say that you feel that $10 would be a fair price for a handmade satchel. In this case, $10 is your negotiation goal. But if you can get it for under $5, that would be a great deal (your negotiation wish). You also determine that you will not pay any more than $12. This is your bottom line.

4. **Open the negotiation at your wish.** If your wish is to buy this product for $5, then it would be in your best interest to open the negotiation at $3 or $4 (a 60 or 70 percent discount to your goal), since the vendor will likely try to haggle up the price. If the vendor asks for $7 instead, you can "compromise" with $5—your original goal.

5. **Be willing to walk away.** This tactic, which we will mention later as a winning tactic in negotiation, applies here as well. When you are willing to walk away, you test the bottom and see how low your counterpart will really go.

6. **Negotiate for a third party.** Tell the vendor that you are shopping for your wife or mom and that you are not sure if they would really like the item or that they told you that you could not spend more than $5. Even people who don't like to negotiate like this strategy because they feel that it is not them asking for a ridiculous price or concession.

7. **Negotiate multiple variables.** When you feel you have gotten the best price the vendor is willing to offer, you can further test the bottom line by asking, "How much lower are you willing to go if I buy two?" Or, "How much of a discount will you give me if I pay all cash?"

8. **Take your time.** If the vendor knows you have a time limit—for example, the sale ends today at 5 p.m. or your cruise ship is leaving port in one hour—they will be less inclined to give you concessions. When time is on your side, you can ask more questions, hold out for a better price, or walk away and find another vendor with similar products.

9. **Stay objective.** Be cautious of vendors who appeal to your emotions. Comments such as "Everyone likes this model best" or "This product looks really good on you" or "You have taken up a lot of my time, you have to buy something" all appeal to your emotions.

10. **Trust, but verify.** Carefully examine what you are going to buy. When emotion kicks in, you tend to overlook details or verify facts. Questions like "Is this a genuine product or a replica?" or "Does this price include tax?" raise important points you want to know prior to buying the product. Once you agree to a sale, most likely every additional deal point will cost you additional money.

Now that you have these ten tips, go out and have fun driving the best possible bargain!

PART II

101 TACTICS FOR SUCCESSFUL NEGOTIATION AND 20 BONUS TACTICS

"Wisdom consists of the anticipation of consequences."

—*Norman Cousins*

U sing words like *strategy* or *tactic* makes some people uncomfortable because they feel these terms suggest manipulation and dishonesty. Nothing could be further from the truth. We do not recommend that you *ever* be dishonest! Being dishonest is not only wrong—it does not build long-term relationships or encourage your counterpart to come back and negotiate with you again at a later date.

Although the terms *strategy* and *tactic* are sometimes used interchangeably, there is a difference. Contemporary dictionaries typically define strategy as a plan for achieving something, particularly over a long period of time, whereas a tactic is most often defined as a device for accomplishing an end. When you combine several tactics in attempting to accomplish your goal, the combined effort becomes your strategy. In other words, a strategy consists of multiple tactics.

You should become familiar with the use of strategies and tactics for two very important reasons. First, everyone uses them on a daily basis. Children, for example, are masters at employing strategies and tactics. Veteran parents have experienced everything from the screaming temper tantrums of a two-year-old to the "silent treatment" of a teenager. These tactics are designed to help kids of different ages achieve their goals.

To demonstrate how tactics permeate our everyday lives, we often present three stages of a scenario in which a couple is deciding where to go out to dinner. Picture yourself in this scenario. How would you respond at the different stages?

1. You get home from work and your significant other says, "Let's go out to dinner" and then suggests a restaurant you do

not enjoy. What do you do or say to convince your partner to go to a different restaurant of your choice? Perhaps you say, "I ate that type of food for lunch." Or "The last time we ate at that restaurant, we had to wait about forty-five minutes to be served." Or "Why don't we go to a place that neither of us has ever been before?"

2. Your significant other replies, "But you chose the restaurant the last time we went out for dinner. It's my turn to choose!" You may suggest, "If you let me choose the restaurant, I'll pay" or "The last time I went to that restaurant, I was on Imodium A-D for three days. I am not going there again."

3. Your significant other remains firm and will not go to another restaurant. She or he touches you gently on the hand and says, "Honey, I was hoping you would go to my restaurant. It would make me so happy." Now what? Would you say, "Okay, let's go" or "Fine, if we can't agree, I'll take you to your restaurant and drop you off. Then I'll go to my restaurant. When I am finished eating, I'll swing by and pick you up"?

In this scenario, both you and your significant other are using tactics to try to accomplish your goal. The point we are making, of course, is that the use of tactics is not something new or unusual. The key thing we have done in this book is not to invent tactics but to describe the ones that are commonly used in negotiations, identify them with a memorable name, tell you how to use them to your advantage, and give you some possible counters (or responses) to employ if someone uses these tactics on you.

And that brings us to the second reason for becoming familiar with common negotiation tactics. Even if you don't like using them yourself, other people will use them in interactions with you. To protect yourself, you need to be able to recognize the tactics and know how to respond to them. Having various counters to employ enables you to retain or regain leverage, or neutralize the tactics used by your counterpart.

The following 101 tactics are commonly used in negotiations. Once you learn to recognize them, you will be able to use them yourself to achieve win-win outcomes—or be prepared to counter them when they are used on you.

1. Is That Your Best Offer?

A great way to practice your negotiation skills is to simply get in the habit of asking salespeople, *"Is That Your Best Offer?"* You would be amazed how many times they will lower their price or throw in an extra benefit in response to this simple question.

EXAMPLE

A buyer is purchasing a new computer from an office supply store and asks the salesperson, "Is $1,299 your best price?" The computer salesperson replies, "This computer is going on sale for $1,199 in a week. Let me see if I can get my manager to approve the sale price for you today." Simply by asking, the buyer saves a hundred dollars.

COUNTER

In this example, the salesperson is honest and does the right thing. The effective counter for this tactic is to build up the value of the benefits that the product or service has to support the price. The salesperson could respond, "That is our best price on this model, but if you do not need the ultra-high-definition in the video card, we can sell you that model over there for $100 less. Which would be better for you?"

2. Referencing an Expert Opinion

One of the more powerful tactics to utilize when presenting information in a negotiation is citing the opinion of an expert.

EXAMPLE

A man is selling his automobile for $20,000. A woman tells him that she will buy the car for $18,500 if she can take it to her mechanic to make sure there are no major problems needing repair. The prospective buyer takes the car to her mechanic, who prepares a computerized printout outlining $1,500 worth of repairs. The buyer returns to the seller with the report and a revised offer to purchase the car for $17,000.

COUNTER

The seller has several possible counters at his disposal in this situation, depending on his goal. If he is confident that a buyer will eventually come along and pay his price, he might simply tell the prospective buyer, "Eighteen-five is the lowest offer I will accept." Second, he could question the validity of the mechanic's recommendations. If the mechanic's report shows the brakes on the truck are bad, the seller may want to go to the trouble of inspecting the brakes himself to test the validity of the report. If the brakes have even ten thousand miles left on them, the seller has more room to negotiate. He can lower the price a bit to cover all or some of the brake repairs, or he can stand firm, saying, "The reason I priced the car so low is that I knew it needed some repairs and I have taken those repairs into account with my asking price." Last, the seller could consider referencing his own expert, taking the car to another mechanic to verify that the prospective buyer's mechanic was accurate on every item that was in need of repair. If the buyer's mechanic was inaccurate on even one item, the strength of this tactic is quickly lost.

3. Asking a Closed-Ended Question

Anytime you are trying to win a concession or gain a deal point in a negotiation, *Asking a Closed-Ended Question* is a good idea. Closed-ended questions are effective because they are direct and to the point. In contrast, they are not good questions to ask when you are striving to build a relationship or stimulate discussion.

EXAMPLE

An employee in charge of office supplies asks a saleswoman, "If I can obtain budget approval to purchase two color copiers that print thirty color pages per minute, have three paper drawers, and have onboard fax and scan features that would normally incur a combined cost of $15,000, can you get the price, with tax, under $14,000 for the pair?"

COUNTER

The saleswoman might ask why the $14,000 figure is so important to the company's budget. A second effective counter would be for the saleswoman to inform the employee that she cannot get the two copiers under $15,000, but if both copiers were purchased for the $15,000 amount, she could include six months of free black-and-white copies, up to ten thousand copies per month, on the contract for both machines.

It is critical for the saleswoman to counter the $14,000 figure. If she concedes to the initial offer and sells the two copiers for $14,000, her counterpart may walk away wondering if he should have offered only $13,500 instead of $14,000.

4. Asking an Open-Ended Question

Open-ended questions almost always start with *who, what, where, when, how,* or *why.* They play a strong role in negotiations as techniques for gaining as much accurate information as possible.

EXAMPLE

Carrie is in the market for a used car. She wants to buy one from someone who has completed the scheduled maintenance. More specifically, she wants to buy a car from someone who has completed routinely scheduled maintenance and changed the oil every five thousand miles. She thinks about *Asking a Closed-Ended Question,* like "Have you changed the oil every five thousand miles?" But since the owner would know the answer Carrie wants to hear, she is afraid he would answer yes even if the real answer were "Yes, when the car was new, but over the last year, the oil has never been changed." She decides to use an open-ended question to gain more complete information and says, "Tell me what type of maintenance has been done on this car." This request has to be answered with details instead of a simple "yes" or "no."

COUNTER

Sometimes you have no idea why a counterpart is asking you a specific question, in which case it may be wise to ask your counterpart a question to clarify or verify why the information is important. For example, the car seller might ask, "Can you tell me what specific type of maintenance records you are interested in reviewing?" Clarifying Carrie's needs may be important, especially if the person selling the car has done all the maintenance himself—and has not kept records. A second counter is to rephrase the question as a closed-ended question and then answer it. For example, the seller could respond, "If you are asking if I have changed the oil regularly, the answer is yes."

5. Concede Small

Here's a good rule of thumb: If you are going to concede in the opening rounds of a negotiation, *Concede Small.*

EXAMPLE

You are selling your house and your asking price is $259,000. You receive an offer of $249,000. Instead of countering with $254,000 in the first round, which is what most people would do, you counter with $257,650. This small concession is a better starting point for this negotiation.

Although negotiating this way takes time, conceding in small increments makes it more likely that you will end up with $254,000. If you immediately counter the buyer's offer at $254,000, he will probably counter with $252,000, and you will end up getting less money for your house.

COUNTER

The best counter for the buyer in this scenario is to respond with his own small concession, for example, a counteroffer of $251,500.

6. Sharing Both Pros and Cons

This tactic is wonderful for promoting full disclosure in a negotiation, and it helps build stronger bonds of trust between counterparts. When you use this tactic, you communicate both the benefits and the possible downsides of a proposal for your counterpart. This tactic is very powerful because you gain points for being honest when it costs you something to do so. Providing the cons usually costs you something.

EXAMPLE

A person is selling a beautiful home with a large yard. When a prospective buyer walks through the home, the Realtor tells the buyer, "The seller has shared with me that his home has a gorgeous view, a beautiful yard, a great school district, and fantastic neighbors. He also said that it comes with a water bill of four hundred dollars per month to support the beautiful yard. He said the water bill was his only surprise when he moved in seven years ago."

COUNTER

The only necessary counter in this situation is for the buyer to do her own research to verify both the pros and cons provided by the seller. When one party in a negotiation utilizes this tactic, the other counterpart may have a tendency to trust the information provided and not feel the need to verify it. In negotiations of significance, everything should be verified.

7. I'll Meet You in the Middle

When two parties are apart on an issue and the negotiation seems to be at a stalemate, one counterpart can offer to split the difference with the other.

EXAMPLE

You are buying a used car and do not want to pay any more than $1,800. The seller does not want to come down any further than $2,000. Since you are $200 apart, either of you could offer to split the difference and do the deal for $1,900.

COUNTER

The rule of thumb in this situation is to let your counterpart offer to split the difference. If you make the offer, your counterpart knows you are willing to pay the higher price. A good solution is to state, "We are only two hundred dollars apart. What should we do?" If the seller offers to split the difference, you know she is willing to accept $1,900. With this new information, you, as the buyer, could counter, "You have just stated that you are willing to take $1,900 for your car. I am willing to give you $1,800. That makes us only $100 apart. Why don't we split the difference and do the deal for $1,850?"

8. Silence Is Golden

When your counterpart is a talker and you want to learn as much as you can about the product, service, or counterpart without making any type of commitment, saying nothing and letting your counterpart do all the talking may be the best tactic. If you do not say anything, there is nothing for the other person to counter.

EXAMPLE

A salesperson is making a presentation on his product. The potential buyer sits and listens to the presentation without saying anything. The salesperson even asks twice if the buyer has any questions about the product. Each time, the buyer just shakes her head no.

COUNTER

The most effective counter for the salesperson would be *Asking an Open-Ended Question* like "How do you plan on utilizing our product?" or "What features about this product are most important to you?" Both these questions force the buyer to dialogue. Without dialogue, it is difficult to build a relationship based on mutual respect.

9. Say "No" and Stick to Your Guns

Sometimes the most effective tactic in a negotiation is simply to say, "No, I am not going to do that" or "That will not work for me."

This is an easy tactic to utilize, although it may be difficult for people who value being nurturing and supportive.

EXAMPLE

A woman is purchasing a flat-screen TV and the salesperson who is writing up the order states, "Almost all our customers find tremendous value and peace of mind by extending the warranty for an additional three years." The woman responds by simply stating, "No, I am not going to do that."

COUNTER

Two counters are possible, and both lead to the same goal. First, the salesperson might ask the woman if she would consider another option, like a two-year extended warranty. Second, he might try *Asking an Open-Ended Question* that would provide him with more information and help him understand why she does not feel the need to extend the warranty. For example, he could ask, "If the screen does malfunction in the next two years, how will you go about getting it repaired?"

10. Wow! You've Got to Be Kidding!

Successful negotiators are good at acting surprised. They communicate the *Wow! You've Got to Be Kidding!* message with a flinch, a sour face, or an expression of disbelief anytime a counterpart mentions the price or conditions of a product or service. We used to think this tactic was rather silly until we realized how effective it was when someone used it on us! Failing to act surprised when price or conditions are mentioned could encourage your counterpart to take advantage of you.

EXAMPLE

A salesperson says, "The price for the brochures will be three thousand dollars for one thousand copies." The client responds, "Wow! You've got to be kidding me! Why so much?"

COUNTER

The salesperson could respond to the client's disbelief with "Of course, that price includes copywriting, photography, graphic design, printing, varnish, and binding."

When someone uses this tactic on you, you have to defend your product or service on its own merit. Many people flinch because they lack knowledge of a product, service, or price. So do not give concessions until you have a solid understanding of why the person flinched. Inexperienced negotiators tend to give up too much too soon.

11. Higher Authority

The tactic of *Higher Authority* can work for either counterpart in a negotiation. Sometimes you cannot get a situation resolved by working with the counterpart assigned to you. Perhaps the counterpart has decided not to comply with your request, or she may not have the authority to fulfill your request. So you have to go to a *Higher Authority* to obtain a satisfactory outcome. On the other hand, lacking the final say in a situation can create a very powerful position for your counterpart, since it provides her with the opportunity to take your request to someone at a higher level in the organization. We have frequently seen experienced negotiators work the best deal they can, then run off to a *Higher Authority* and come back with instructions for an even better deal.

EXAMPLE

A real estate developer requests a line of credit from his local bank branch. The branch manager says that the loan has been denied by the loan committee (the *Higher Authority*) at the bank. The developer asks if there is anything he can do to have his loan reconsidered. The branch manager apologizes, but says there is nothing she can do once the committee has denied a loan.

COUNTER

Since the branch manager is denying that she can do anything to help the developer, he could counter by going over her head, using the tactic of the *Higher Authority* himself. He could call the bank president or a member of the loan committee and ask that his loan be reconsidered. In the above example, the bank president might request that the branch manager repackage the real estate developer's loan so it could be approved.

The best way to keep the tactic of the *Higher Authority* from being used on you in the first place is to ask your counterpart in the very beginning whether she is the person who makes the final decision. If not, ask to make your presentation to the decision maker.

12. Good Guy/Bad Guy

The *Good Guy/Bad Guy* technique is very similar to the tactic of the *Higher Authority* but is much more specific. With *Good*

Guy/Bad Guy, one person pretends to be on your side and appears to help you make the deal. But every time you strike a deal, the good guy marches off to the bad guy for final approval. Naturally, the bad guy will renegotiate the deal you have worked out with the good guy. Anytime you get into this scenario and do not expose the technique, you can end up with devastating consequences.

EXAMPLE

If you have ever bought a new car, most likely you have experienced the frustration of being in a *Good Guy/Bad Guy* situation. After you have test-driven the car, the salesperson takes you into the closing room to draw up the initial deal. Since the salesperson cannot approve anything himself, he marches off to the sales manager to get the manager's input on the deal. It is the job of the sales manager to rewrite the deal to get more money for the dealership. Then the salesperson returns and says that you are close, but the original deal will not work. What is scary is that dealerships go through this process whether your offer is a good one or a bad one.

COUNTER

First, you can fight fire with fire. The last time I bought a new car, I took my wife. Every time the salesperson went off to the sales manager, I took the deal to my wife (who was in the lobby) to review it. At one point, when the salesperson told me we had a deal, but he would have to raise the price of the car five hundred dollars, I replied that we had a real problem because my wife had said I couldn't do the deal at the previous price unless I could get the interest rate down another point.

Second, you can expose the technique. Tell your counterpart that you do not appreciate the *Good Guy/Bad Guy* routine. I once told a salesperson that if he did not have enough authority to make the deal, he should bring in someone who did. I warned that the next time he left the room, I would also leave. Keep in mind that if the salesperson needs to get approval from the sales manager, he can make a phone call with you in the room.

13. That's Not Good Enough

The idea behind this tactic is very simple. When someone makes you an offer you think could be improved, you simply respond, *"That's Not Good Enough."* Then pause and let your counterpart make the next response.

EXAMPLE

An employee, after working hard on a particularly complicated report, gave it to his boss for review. His boss, without looking at the report, said, "Is this your best work?" The employee thought for a moment and, worried that his boss would think the report was not good enough, responded, "Let me review it one more time." One week later, the employee turned in the revised report. This time the boss kept the report for a week, then returned it to the employee with a note that said, "Are you sure this is your best work?" Realizing that something must have been missing, the employee once again reviewed and rewrote parts of the report. This time when he handed the report to his boss, he said, "I'm sure this is my best work." Hearing that, the boss replied, "Then this time I will read your report."

COUNTER

The best counter for the employee in this situation would have been to gain more information by *Asking an Open-Ended Question* like "Is there anything you were specifically looking for in my report that is not there?" or "Is there anything specific about my report that you do not like?" or "Just out of curiosity, why are you asking about the quality of my work?" or "How do you define 'best work'?" The key to countering the tactic is not divulging information until it is clear what is being asked.

14. Facts and Statistics

Anytime you can incorporate *Facts and Statistics* into your presentation, you have a tool that your counterpart will find difficult to handle. Reliable facts can add a tremendous amount of power and credibility to your case. But be careful—if you quote statistics incorrectly and your counterpart proves you wrong, you lose your credibility. Once this happens, you have to fight twice as hard to gain any deal point.

EXAMPLE

An employee goes to his boss with a recently published salary survey documenting that the employee's salary is significantly below market. The employee has pulled *Facts and Statistics* that examine salary levels by industry, position, and geographic location to demonstrate the discrepancy.

COUNTER

First, the boss could question the validity of the employee's *Facts and Statistics*. Who participated in the salary survey? Who collected the information? Are the salary statistics valid for someone with this employee's experience? Has the salary survey been done in this industry and location, or somewhere else?

As a second option, the boss could delay the negotiation process to give himself time to do some research and develop his own *Facts and Statistics*.

15. Trade-off Concession

A good rule to remember in negotiation is to get something in return every time you give up something. Once you give up a deal point, it has very little value later in the negotiation.

EXAMPLE

A home buyer states, "I will buy your house for $280,000, but for that price, you will have to throw in your refrigerator, washer, and dryer." The seller responds, "I will throw in my refrigerator, washer, and dryer, but if I do that, you will have to close escrow in thirty days." Or "I will throw in my refrigerator, washer, and dryer, but you will have to pay $282,000."

If the seller does not get a trade-off every time she makes a concession, her counterpart will most likely ask for more concessions. Then if the seller suddenly says, "Wait a moment. I already gave you a washer, dryer, and refrigerator, and now you are asking for more concessions," the buyer can respond, "Why are you bringing up the washer, dryer, and refrigerator? We already agreed to that."

COUNTER

The buyer might respond to the seller's counteroffer with yet another deal point. For example, he could say, "If you throw in the refrigerator, washer, and dryer, I will agree to close escrow in thirty days, but you will have to agree to complete all the repairs identified in the home inspection report."

When using the *Trade-off Concession* tactic, the following are good rules to keep in mind.

- If you can, encourage your counterpart to concede first.
- Exchange concessions for deal points that have less value to you, but greater value to your counterpart.
- Concede in small increments.
- Consider phrases like "I'll consider it" and "Let me think about that." Just *Say No and Stick to Your Guns* if the concession is not in your best interests.
- Do not concede anything without getting something in return. Your counterpart will have more appreciation for the final outcome and more respect for you.

16. The Ultimatum

From time to time, it may be in your best interest to "draw a line in the sand," or create a rule that allows you to hold your counterpart accountable. One tactic you can use is to tell your counterpart the actions you will take if your conditions are not met.

EXAMPLE

A client calls a consulting firm and asks to tentatively reserve a date for a seminar to be presented at her company in approximately six months. Three months before the date in question, the consulting firm calls the client and asks her to confirm the reserved date or the firm will have to offer it to another client who has requested the same day. The client is told that a confirmation is needed within twenty-four hours, which makes the deadline her *Ultimatum*.

COUNTER

If you wish to complete a deal but need more time to get permissions or approvals, one of the most effective counters to the *Ultimatum* is postponement. In this specific example, the client might respond that she cannot get the date confirmed within the twenty-four-hour time frame, but she can have an answer within forty-eight hours, and ask if that would be acceptable.

If the deal outcome is not important to her and she needs more time to get approvals, she can simply walk away and find another seminar provider.

17. Sweetening the Deal

At times you may need to add a little something "extra" to make a deal work. For example, a salesperson may increase or decrease the price of a product, add a warranty or training at no additional charge, or agree to extend a sale price to make a deal more enticing. This tactic of offering an extra or add-on is called *Sweetening the Deal*.

EXAMPLE

A customer tells a carpet saleswoman, "Your carpet is a dollar per yard more expensive than your competitor's." The seller *Sweetens the Deal* by saying, "I will carpet each of your closets for free if you will sign the contract today."

COUNTER

The *Trade-off Concession* could work well here. The customer might reply, "I will sign the contract today if you carpet the closets for free and can have the carpet installed by Friday of this week." From the salesperson's point of view, an effective counter to the customer's counter would be "I can install the carpet by Friday, but if you are looking for the highest-quality installation, keep in mind that my best installers will not be available until next Wednesday. Will that work for you?"

18. Clarifying the Ground Rules

Although creating ground rules for conducting a negotiation is not necessary with the majority of counterparts, it may sometimes be in your best interest to do so.

EXAMPLE

At a negotiation between the union and management team of a Fortune 100 company, the union president and twenty-five of his closest friends showed up to negotiate. There were so many sidebar conversations and comments made by people not leading the negotiation that it was difficult to tell who was really in charge of the union's team. Just as management started to make progress, someone on the union team would disagree. In this case, the first issue that should have been negotiated was how many players each team could have in the room at one time and who would be allowed to speak on behalf of each team.

COUNTER

Keep in mind, ground rules are negotiable. In a negotiation, both sides have to go in with high aspirations in order to create a win-win outcome. Either counterpart could lose a negotiation by giving up a small point, like how many people are allowed to attend the meeting. Ground rules, when set properly, should help both counterparts ensure success.

19. Moving the Goalpost

Sometimes you will be unable to accomplish your negotiation goal. In those instances, it may be best to quickly switch goals. In almost every negotiation, there is a need to change tactics or strategies. For example, if you are getting a bid to have your house painted and the painting company quotes a price that seems too high to you, you may first try the tactic of *Wow! You've Got to Be Kidding!* If that doesn't work, you may try to support your offer with *Facts and Statistics*. But if both these tactics are unsuccessful and you realize your original goal is unobtainable, you may need to change your goal.

EXAMPLE

An individual buys a two-thousand-dollar couch from a furniture warehouse. When the couch is delivered, the buyer finds out that its springs make exceedingly annoying squeaks whenever

anyone sits down. The initial goal of the buyer is to get the furniture warehouse to replace the couch with a new one. But when
the buyer calls, the manager states that the company is going out
of business, so all sales are final, which was noted in the contract.
All the tactics the buyer has initially planned to use (e.g., stress-
ing the value of a long-term relationship, threatening to report
the company to the Better Business Bureau) will be useless, since
the seller has no commitment to the relationship. The buyer then
switches her position by asking, "If you will not replace the couch,
will you at least come to my home and see if there is anything you
can do to fix the squeaks?" The seller agrees. After examining the
problem, the manager puts the buyer in contact with the manufacturer, who agrees to send out a service technician to fix the
problem or replace the couch.

COUNTER

The most effective protection when a counterpart switches goals
or tries a new tactic on you is to have a very clear picture of the
outcome you need to create a win-win situation. When you have
a firm bottom line, you cannot be taken advantage of. In the example above, agreeing to send someone to look at the couch was
not a problem for the seller, so a counter was not needed.

20. Isolating Agreement

In complex negotiations, there are usually many deal points
that need to be discussed and negotiated. Issues such as price,
delivery schedules, service agreements, warranty, who will actually perform the work, training, and how "add-ons" or addi-

tional work will be handled are all examples of negotiable issues that need to be determined. If both parties are close to agreement on these issues, it may be best to discuss them first in the negotiation.

EXAMPLE

When unions and management teams negotiate, they almost always negotiate the easiest points up front, and then save the economic issues for the very last. This serves two purposes. First, it speeds up the negotiation by getting resolution to the issues on which both parties agree. Second, it helps build the relationship between counterparts by allowing them to reach agreement on the easier issues.

COUNTER

There are two important points to remember if you or your counterpart uses this tactic. First, you should not narrow the negotiation down to one last issue. If you do, you may create a win-lose outcome. For example, when wages are the last thing left on the table, neither side has much room left for negotiation.

Second, when using this tactic, remember, a lose-lose outcome is always a possibility. For example, if wages are the last deal point to be negotiated and the management team finally agrees to the union's demands for higher wages but then has to lay off people because they can't run a profitable business by paying the higher wages, both sides lose.

One effective defense against *Isolating Agreement* is to tackle the toughest topic first. Doing so ensures that you have additional deal points you can juggle to create a win-win outcome.

21. Putting the Most Difficult Issue Last

With this tactic, *Isolating Agreement* is taken to the extreme and the single most difficult issue is left for last. One example of an issue that is often the last to be negotiated is indemnification. When major corporations with deep pockets (e.g., utilities) negotiate contracts, they want to be indemnified, to avoid liability and prevent a lawsuit if any of their contractors' products or services fail.

EXAMPLE

A utility wishes to purchase a transformer from a manufacturer. Everything is negotiated, including the price and delivery dates. The last thing to be negotiated is the indemnification clause, and that is where the negotiation falls apart. The manufacturer insists that its legal department will not approve the indemnification clause as it is written, and the utility says it cannot purchase the equipment without the indemnification.

COUNTER

The most effective way to avoid this situation is to put the most difficult deal point first. We have worked with large corporations that have used this tactic: They have called manufacturers that have been resistant to indemnify in the past and said, "We are in the process of putting together a list of vendors to whom to send a 'request for proposal.' There is a problem. On this particular product we are buying, we need you to agree to full indemnification. If you would like to submit a proposal, you need to send us a letter informing us that you agree to indemnify the utility and hold us harmless. If this is a problem, we understand your position, but we will not send you a request for proposal." In this example, the corporation put the most difficult deal point first.

22. The Safeguard

The Safeguard is employed when a relationship is new or you have little or no trust in it. The tactic is designed to protect you in the event that your counterpart does not live up to his negotiated deal point.

EXAMPLE

A retailer or distributor offers to buy 50,000 units from a manufacturer for $1 per unit. The normal cost for anything less than 50,000 units is $1.25 per unit. The manufacturer agrees to the $1 price but places a *Safeguard* into the contract that reads, "In the event that the distributor does not purchase 50,000 units by the end of the year, she will be back-billed 25 cents per unit." Or the manufacturer stipulates that if the distributor has not ordered 50,000 units by the end of the year, the price effective in the new year will be $1.25 per unit. Both of these examples provide *Safeguards* to the manufacturer.

COUNTER

There are three effective counters the distributor could employ: (1) She could just *Say "No" and Stick to Her Guns*; (2) she could argue that her corporation has a policy that does not allow any type of back-billing; or (3) if she is interested in building a long-term relationship, she could negotiate a "tiered" price, agreeing to pay, for example, $1.35 per unit for orders up to 20,000, $1.15 per unit for additional units up to 40,000, and $1 per unit on any purchase over 40,000. Although "sharks" might debate the wisdom of this last counter, being friendly and flexible helps build relationships. People are much more willing to help create a win-win outcome with a counterpart they like and trust.

23. Uncovering the Real Reason

Many negotiators listen to their counterparts tell them why their proposal will not work, but never get to the real reason for the counterpart's blocking or rejecting the proposal. To be an effective negotiator, you have to learn to *Uncover the Real Reason* behind a counterpart's resistance.

EXAMPLE

Jack is refinancing a home. His mortgage broker itemizes all the charges that will be associated with securing a new loan. Jack asks his broker if the fee for the appraisal of the house can be waived since he had an appraisal done on the house six months earlier and would like to use that appraisal. The mortgage broker refuses, saying that getting an appraisal is standard company policy and her boss would never approve of waiving the appraisal or the fee. In this situation, to find out if there is another reason the broker does not want to waive the fee, it would be appropriate for Jack to ask if he could speak directly to the broker's boss. If the explanation the broker has given Jack is not exactly accurate, the broker will probably make a concession. Better yet, if she does let Jack talk to her boss, he may succeed in gaining something he would not have gained if he had not used this tactic.

COUNTER

The mortgage broker has three possible counters. The first is to provide detailed information about why this deal point is critical to the success of both parties in this negotiation. If this tactic is successful, the negotiation will continue.

A second effective counter is to come up with options. The mortgage broker could suggest that, instead of doing a full appraisal with a complete walk-through of the house, the appraiser might do a drive-by appraisal. A mini-appraisal would help lower the costs.

A third counter could be the tactic of the *Higher Authority* and would sound like this: "On the off chance that I could get my boss to waive the appraisal fee in this situation, would you like me to ask her?" This leaves the situation in the broker's control and gives her the opportunity to approach her boss with the request. Then she can go back to Jack and waive the fee entirely, waive part of the fee, or say something like "I did speak to my boss and she said that the company's policy makes waiving the fee nonnegotiable."

24. Would You Like the "Meal Deal"?

One of the challenges everyone has faced is the aggressive salesperson who receives a commission if he sells additional products or services, such as an extended warranty. The perfect model of this tactic is the fast-food cashier who always asks, "Would you like fries with your hamburger?" and attempts to "upsell" you on the "Meal Deal" instead of the simple hamburger you originally ordered, telling you that you'll get more food, a drink, and will save money with the meal.

EXAMPLE

Sue is buying a new tablet and the salesperson says, "You really should purchase the extended warranty. If anything goes wrong, like the screen breaking, we will replace it free of charge." The salesperson convinces Sue to buy the extended warranty, just as she would buy a life insurance policy, with the argument, "You just never know."

Some people like extended warranties; others feel such warranties are a waste of money. Some individuals have purchased the warranties and, when the product has malfunctioned, have been unable to find the paperwork, so the retail chain would not honor the warranty anyway. Or the extended warranty seems to cover almost everything except what you need fixed.

COUNTER

There are three effective counters. We learned one from an elderly gentleman. When a salesperson asked the seventy-five-year-old man if he wanted an extended warranty on his new washing machine, the man replied, "Son, at my age, I don't even buy green bananas."

When the dollar value of the product being purchased is low, a second effective counter is to reply, "When this product breaks, I'll just throw it out and buy another." This counter is not bad logic when the price of the product and the cost of the extended warranty are factored in.

The last tactic requires a little more confidence. Sue can look the salesperson in the eye and say, "You are putting a lot of emphasis on selling me an extended warranty. I like buying quality products that do not break. Are you trying to indirectly tell me this product is not reliable and I need some insurance?"

25. Focusing on the Future

Sometimes counterparts get into conflict and start blaming each other for negative things that have happened in the past. (This is as common in marriage as it is in long-term business relationships!) Getting stuck in the past can make it very difficult to create a win-win outcome, since all the negotiators are busy blaming their counterparts or defending themselves. Under these circumstances, it may be in your best interest to *Focus on the Future*.

EXAMPLE

A manager is counseling an employee about poor performance on the job. Each time the manager brings up an example of the employee's poor performance, the employee blames the specific problem on the manager or another department. Since difficult employees will defend their wrongful actions to their death, it is helpful to *Focus on the Future*. It would be appropriate for the manager to ask the difficult employee, "What will it take to have you produce a quality product next week?" Even the most difficult employees will help define the future.

COUNTER

If you are put in this situation and, for some reason, do not want to be held completely accountable for the results of the negotiation, the appropriate counter is the tactic of the *Safeguard*. In the example above, the employee might reply, "I will do what I can to produce a quality product next week, but if I do not get all the information and cooperation I need from other departments, I may not be able to accomplish that goal.

26. Forgive Me, for I Have Sinned

The ability to say "I am sorry" or "I made a mistake" is a strength, not a weakness. When you are humble, your counterpart finds it easier to like you and work with you to create a win-win outcome.

EXAMPLE

A book printing representative receives a large order from a client. The books are supposed to be completed by a specific date, but something happens at the printing plant and the delivery is late. The client is disappointed and is not planning to use the same company to print her books in the future. But the sales representative makes a special trip to the client's company to personally apologize for the tardiness of the delivery. The sales representative's obviously sincere apology convinces the client to continue to utilize the printing company's services.

COUNTER

In this situation, the damage has been done. It would be appropriate for the client to accept the sales representative's apology and then put a *Safeguard* in place to guide the future relationship. For example, "If you are ever late on one of my jobs again, I will not accept delivery." *Safeguards* are negotiated so that remedies are in place in case the problem ever recurs in the relationship. The client could also negotiate an add-on, or something extra, for the inconvenience.

27. Deflecting an Answer with a Great Question

It may not be in your best interest to answer a counterpart's question if you do not have enough information to make an educated or appropriate response. In those situations, *Deflecting an Answer with a Great Question* is appropriate.

EXAMPLE

A salesperson asks you, "If I could get this model in the Titanium Frost Metallic color that you like so well, would you be willing to purchase the car today?" You respond by stating, "How long would it take you to locate the model in the right color, with all the options I want, and have it delivered?" You have not made a commitment, and at the same time you have asked a great question, which could yield information important to your purchasing decision. When negotiating to buy something, you can almost always make more gains before committing to buy than you can afterward.

COUNTER

If someone uses this tactic on you, the counter is to answer the question to the best of your ability and confirm that your answer is acceptable to your counterpart. Once you have agreement or understanding, return to *Asking Your Closed-Ended Question* to gain commitment to buy: "If I can have the model in the color you want, with all the options you have picked, delivered by this weekend, would you be willing to complete the purchase order today?"

28. Calling Your Bluff

Once in a while, one party to a negotiation may say something outrageous in the belief that his counterpart does not have enough information to challenge him. The appropriate tactic in this situation is to simply call your counterpart's bluff.

EXAMPLE

Maria is trying to sell her car. A potential buyer offers her $1,500 less than her asking price. Maria justifies her asking price by telling the buyer, "I've already had an offer at my original asking price." The buyer calls her bluff, asking, "Why didn't you sell your car to the buyer with the higher offer?" This is a great question, since it will probably help *Uncover the Real Reason* the car is still available and Maria is still negotiating.

A second common example is a slight variation. A person buying a product might say, "I don't even need your product." Once again, the appropriate question is "If you do not need my product, why are you even taking the time to talk with me?"

COUNTER

You do not need a counter to this tactic if you are negotiating honestly and providing full disclosure. In the event that a counterpart tries *Calling Your Bluff* with a good question, simply reply, "That's a great question," and give the honest reason why you are negotiating with him.

29. If You Were in My Shoes

Once in a while, your counterpart will ask for something that is totally unreasonable or does not make good business sense to you. In this situation, a great question to ask is "How would you justify your request or agree to your position *If You Were in My Shoes?*"

EXAMPLE

Two companies were in serious talks regarding a merger. Company A wanted Company B to agree to the following deal point: If the news of the merger became public and another merger bid was generated from a third company, Company B would pay Company A $1 million if the original merger failed to happen. When the president of Company A proposed this deal point, the president of Company B asked this great question: *"If You Were in My Shoes,* how would you justify agreeing to that position?" What usually happens when this tactic is used is that the counterpart who is the target of the tactic has to pause and think how he would justify his position. In the example above, if the president of Company A paused for a long time, or avoided the question altogether, the president of Company B could have pointed out, "I'm having the same challenge figuring out how this deal works for me."

COUNTER

The most effective counter for the president of Company A would have been to present *Facts and Statistics* that supported his position to explain how that position could be justified.

30. I Feel Your Pain

A counterpart who feels you do not understand his feelings, needs, or goals may build up a defensive wall. Breaking through that wall could make the negotiation take two or three times as long to reach a resolution. It is also possible that you might not succeed in breaking through the wall at all. Sometimes you are better off letting go of the facts in a negotiation and focusing on the emotions behind the facts. A counterpart who believes you are really listening to his needs and goals and understand how he feels is more willing to cooperate with you.

EXAMPLE

We were hired by a school district to resolve a dispute it was having with some parents. The dispute revolved around the fact that a group of special needs preschoolers was left unsupervised on a playground. Although the lack of supervision was less than a few minutes, and the play area was fully fenced, the preschoolers' parents were angry about the lack of supervision. They were especially angry because they felt that everyone who represented the school district was busy documenting facts to "play it safe," and no one really cared about the parents' concerns. We began to facilitate the negotiation by listening to the parents express their concerns for nearly two hours. Then our first words to them were "We have children, too, and we can understand why you are upset." The parents responded, "We would not have made such a case out of this situation if someone had listened to us as you just did."

COUNTER

One tactic to utilize is *If You Were in My Shoes*. In this case, the parents could have said, "If you really understand how we feel, tell us how you would handle the situation if you were in our position."

Another tactic is to make a call for action: "We appreciate the fact that you understand how we feel. That is important. It is equally important that we come to a decision about what action needs to be taken to ensure that this type of situation never arises again."

31. Playing a Broken Record

One of the most difficult negotiators to deal with is the unilateral thinker who can see only one possible outcome to a negotiation. This negotiator's attitude is "My way or the highway."

EXAMPLE

An airline passenger is irate because the first-class reservation she thought was confirmed for her flight is not in the airline's system and no other first-class seats are available. To every option the reservations specialist suggests, the woman reiterates, "My reservation is in the system. You have to find my seat."

COUNTER

There are several counters that may be effective in this situation. Apologizing and responding to the customer's frustration with empathy is a great place to start. Brainstorming alternative solutions with the passenger or suggesting other alternatives that might work could also be effective. For example, since no first-class seats are available, the airline employee might offer the passenger a seat in a section of coach that is close to the front of the plane. She might also try the tactic of *Higher Authority* by asking, "On the off chance that my supervisor can find you a first-class seat on another flight, would that be agreeable to you?"

But some people never stop *Playing Their Broken Record*. If that is the case, the airline employee could acknowledge the passenger's emotions (using the tactic of *I Feel Your Pain*) and simply say, "I understand this is a very frustrating situation and you are not happy. Of the possible solutions I have suggested, which one would work best for you?"

32. Launching a Tangent

There are times when a counterpart specializes in inserting into a negotiation a tangent, or side issue, that has absolutely nothing to do with the negotiation being discussed.

EXAMPLE

A manager is discussing with an employee the importance of coming to work on time. In the middle of the discussion, the employee protests, "Other employees come into work late and you do not say anything to them." This is an example of *Launching a Tangent* to deflect attention from the real issue, this employee's continual tardiness.

COUNTER

The most effective counter in this situation is to employ the tactic of *Deflecting an Answer with a Great Question* and then get back to the agenda. For example, it would be appropriate for the manager to ask, "What makes you believe I do not give other employees who come into work late the courtesy of dealing with them one-on-one, just as I am doing with you?" or "If I allow you to come into work late but I do not allow other employees to do so, is it possible some people may think I am playing favorites with you?" Then the manager could continue, "What do you think you could do differently to enable you to get to work on time each day?"

33. I'll Think About It and Get Back to You Later

One of the tactics that can keep the door open in a negotiation is: *"I'll Think About It and Get Back to You Later."*

EXAMPLE

A yacht broker knows that his client is very interested in the model he is showing her. The Bay Cruiser has everything the client is looking for, and is priced fairly. The broker asks, "Will you be able to come up with a down payment of ten percent of the asking price if I help you secure financing for the asking price?" The buyer responds, "That is a great question. I need to think about it, talk it over with my husband, and *I'll Get Back to You Later.*"

COUNTER

Some questions a counterpart could ask to counter this tactic would be "What specifically are you going to think about or talk over with your husband?" and "When will you get back to me?" Another appropriate response for the broker would be to explain that, until the buyer gets back to him, he will continue to show the boat and seek other offers. Finally, a more aggressive response would be to ask, "Why do you need to think about how much you have for the down payment? Do you have a ballpark figure in mind that we could discuss?"

34. Whatever

With this tactic, one counterpart appears to be uninterested in the outcome of the negotiation. She simply encourages the other counterpart to follow through with the terms. Her attitude is clearly, "*Whatever . . .*"

EXAMPLE

Company A warns Company B that if a delinquent bill is not paid, Company A will turn the matter over to a collection agency and proceed with litigation. The representative for Company B replies, "We are already being sued by six other companies. Next week we are planning to file for bankruptcy. We will provide you with the name and address of our bankruptcy attorney and you can send the collection paperwork directly to him. Perhaps that will save you some time."

A second example is a parent giving a teenager some tough feedback about a bad report card. The parent says, "If you don't improve your grades, you will be grounded indefinitely and not get your driver's license." The teenager replies, *"Whatever,* I don't care. I don't have any friends or anyplace I want to go anyway."

COUNTER

In the first example, although Company A's goal, getting the money, remains the same, it will most likely be in the company's best interest to switch tactics. First, Company A could utilize the tactic of *Calling Your Bluff* and ask for the name and address of Company B's bankruptcy attorney. If there really is no bankruptcy attorney to communicate with, Company A may want to stay on the collection course. If it seems the debt is eventually going to fall into the bankruptcy courts, it may be in Company A's best interest to use the tactic of *Moving the Goalpost,* agreeing to accept a lesser amount if the account is settled immediately. Receiving seventy cents on the dollar today is almost always better than waiting for a court to decide.

Every parent wants to know the counter to the second example! Although it is impossible to predict every child's reaction, we have two suggestions. First, the parent could ask the teen a great question like "If you are grounded indefinitely and you get asked to the prom, how will you feel when you can't go?" A second possible tactic is *Calling Your Bluff.* The parent could respond, "Great! At least I will know where to find you until your grades improve."

35. Establishing a Fair Starting Point

Negotiations generally benefit from having a starting point both counterparts consider fair.

EXAMPLE

Two business partners enter a buy-sell agreement that *Establishes a Fair Starting Point* in case either partner wants to buy the other partner out in the future. They make the following agreement, sometimes referred to as a "Dutch Auction": If Partner 1 wants to buy out Partner 2, Partner 1 will make an offer that he considers fair and acceptable. Partner 2 is then given a choice. She can accept Partner 1's offer, or reverse the offer and buy out Partner 1 under the same terms. This system of *Establishing a Fair Starting Point* encourages any partner interested in buying out another partner's interest to make a fair and reasonable offer.

COUNTER

The so-called Dutch auction, if drawn up by an attorney, is a difficult tactic to counter because both parties agree to the fair starting point before the tactic is ever utilized.

36. Making the First Offer

Some negotiators believe you should *never* make the first offer. We have watched negotiations stall because neither counterpart was willing to make the initial move. We believe that if you have conducted thorough research, planned well, set high aspirations, and made a commitment to a win-win outcome, you should have no fears about *Making the First Offer*. The only time we would discourage you from doing so is when you have no interest in what is being negotiated.

EXAMPLE

Two couples are out for dinner one evening. John and Mary announce that they are planning to sell their home. Mark and Elizabeth state, "We love your home and want to buy it. What is your price?" John and Mary respond, "Based on a competitive market analysis completed by two different real estate brokers, we feel a fair price is $350,000." John and Mary have done their homework and have high aspirations, so there is no reason for them to hesitate to make the first offer.

COUNTER

There are several effective counters for this example. One possible counter is the tactic *Wow! You've Got to Be Kidding!* This would be especially appropriate if Mark and Elizabeth's banker has told them that the maximum loan they could qualify for is $325,000. A second effective counter would be for Mark and Elizabeth to conduct their own competitive market analysis and counter with a lower price, using the tactic of *Facts and Statistics*. If they are not clear about how the price was determined, a third counter could be the tactic of *Asking an Open-Ended Question:* "Just so we understand, what comparable neighborhood and homes did the real estate brokers use in their competitive market analysis?"

37. There Is More Than One Way to Cook an Egg

In a negotiation, the counterpart with the greatest number of viable options usually gets the best outcome. A good tactic is to walk into a negotiation with three to five possibilities for accomplishing your goal. This tactic empowers you because when your counterpart puts a roadblock in one direction, you have other viable alternatives.

Some of the most difficult negotiators to deal with are unilateral thinkers who believe there is only one way to do things. When one counterpart won't look at options, the negotiation is likely to result in a lose-win outcome.

EXAMPLE

You would like to hire a star salesperson for your company. Your boss has enforced a salary ceiling of $100,000 for the position. But during an interview, you discover that the salesperson you want to hire has a base salary of $110,000 at her current job and will not leave for less.

You reopen the negotiations with a different proposal. You offer the salesperson a base salary of $100,000 but promise to give a $25,000 bonus if she can reach sales of $500,000. This arrangement is more acceptable to your boss, and the salesperson thinks she will have no problem selling $500,000 worth of your product.

COUNTER

The salesperson could use the tactic of *I'll Think About It and Get Back to You Later*, to have time to evaluate the new proposal. If her goals and yours are still some distance apart, she could try *I'll Meet You in the Middle*.

38. Moving the Deadline

Since many negotiators set a deadline for making a decision, it is important to note that almost every deadline can be moved. Instead of hastily making a bad decision "under the gun" of a deadline, consider changing it.

EXAMPLE

A salesperson tells a potential buyer that the sale price on a particular product will be available only until the end of the month. The buyer explains, "That is too bad because I do not get paid until the fifth of next month and all my credit cards are maxed out. Is it possible that on this one item you could get management's approval to give me a rain check on the sale price until the fifth?"

COUNTER

The salesperson could counter this tactic by protesting that his company has a formal written policy of not extending the sale price on items, since doing so would mean that everything in the store would be on sale all the time! A second effective counter is the tactic of *There Is More Than One Way to Cook an Egg*. The salesperson could offer the option of a layaway, writing up the sale today but setting the product aside until the fifth. This would accomplish both counterparts' goals.

39. Take It or Leave It

An effective tactic used by negotiators is saying, "This is our best and final offer. *Take It or Leave It*." This tactic, which is commonly used by labor unions, is designed to discourage additional negotiation. Making a fixed offer sends the message that if the counterpart does not agree, there will be no further discussion. A real test of egos ensues when a counterpart replies, "We'll leave it. We are walking out of the negotiations."

EXAMPLE

The mechanics at a major airline have gone without a contract for several years because the mechanics' union and management have not been able to agree on salary. Finally, the union demands a salary package and says, "That is our best offer. *Take It or Leave It.*"

COUNTER

One effective counter to *Take It or Leave It* is *Deflecting an Answer with a Great Question.* In the example above, management might ask, "What will happen if we do not get this dispute resolved?" This tactic is designed to force the union negotiators to face the consequences of management's walking out of the negotiation. A second option might be to use the tactic of *Calling Your Bluff.* Management could walk out or tell the union leaders, "Okay, then, you might as well leave now." The effectiveness of this tactic depends on which side is least committed to the relationship. Another possible tactic is *Asking an Open-Ended Question* to verify the validity of the union's threat. For example, the airline negotiator might ask, "If you strike, what action do you think the federal government will take?" Finally, management could simply ignore the union's *Take It or Leave It* tactic and continue negotiating. This is probably the best approach when the goal is to build a win-win relationship based on trust.

40. The Trial Balloon

Finding out how firm your counterpart is on the key issues is often helpful in a negotiation. You can get some information by sending up a *Trial Balloon* and watching your counterpart's reaction. This tactic may give you a better understanding of what to expect when you get down to doing the final negotiation.

EXAMPLE

A home seller is asking $250,000 for her house. The buyer's agent presents a cash offer of $230,000 with a thirty-day escrow.

COUNTER

In this example, the *Wow! You've Got to Be Kidding!* tactic could prove effective. A second effective counter could be the response *That's Not Good Enough.* A third possible counter could be to support the $250,000 asking price with *Facts and Statistics,* citing the selling price for comparable homes in the neighborhood.

41. If . . . Then

This tactic, which is similar to the *Trial Balloon,* is used to check out your counterpart's acceptance of your proposal. This tactic is based on the idea that most people never give up anything without getting something in return.

EXAMPLE

You are a salesperson. A potential buyer asks you, "If I am willing to sign the purchase order today for five hundred units, then would you be willing to lower the price by one hundred dollars per unit?"

COUNTER

Before accepting an *If . . . Then* offer, make sure that what you are agreeing to is in your long-term best interest. You may want to reverse the tactic, asking your counterpart, "If I do lower the price, then will you also be willing to make each payment 'net ten'?" A second tactic may be to buy more time to research the long-term value, using the *I'll Think About It and Get Back to You Later* tactic: "Before I agree to lower the price by that much, I need to think it over and do more financial projections. I will get back to you next week."

42. Feeling Hurt or Betrayed

Most negotiators want to avoid hurting someone else's feelings. Tough negotiators don't mind being ruthless, since they consider their actions just a part of business, but even they don't feel comfortable when someone tells them they have hurt his feelings or betrayed him in some way.

EXAMPLE

We were negotiating a subcontract for our services. In the middle of the negotiation, the contractor stopped and stated that it was important that we know how he felt. He went on to tell us that because of our long business relationship, he felt hurt and betrayed that we would not work for him unless we made a higher fee. We backed up and changed our aspirations because we felt terrible that he was taking our actions so personally. We do not mind driving a hard bargain, but we do not want to hurt people's feelings in the process. Unfortunately, we learned when this happened a second time with the same person that the "hurt feelings" was just a tactic.

COUNTER

We could have simply apologized and asked the contractor to clarify why he felt hurt. Or it may have been helpful to ask, *"If You Were in Our Shoes,* could you understand why obtaining the higher fee might be important to us?"

43. Find Us an Umpire

When two counterparts do not have a history of working well together, using an intermediary or "umpire" to facilitate the negotiation can sometimes prove helpful. In this case, a third party who has had previous positive relationships with both counterparts enters the picture.

EXAMPLE

Two corporate presidents know it is in the best interests of both their companies to merge. In fact, they know that if they continue on the present course, they will both eventually be leading unprofitable companies. The problem is that they have met twice before to negotiate a merger. Since each of them has an ego the size of King Kong, they have left the table without a deal each time, and their relationship has ended up even more strained. A vendor who sells machinery to both companies and is well liked by both presidents enters the picture. This vendor starts to talk with each president separately about merging the companies and eventually brings the two presidents face-to-face to create a win-win outcome.

COUNTER

Of course, an obvious counter would be for one counterpart to refuse to work with a mediator, but in this example, countering would not be in either president's best interest.

If you agree to work with a mediator in a negotiation, we have two helpful suggestions. First, make sure you verify that the mediator chosen is truly impartial, and does not unfairly represent one side. Test the information the mediator presents for accuracy. If necessary, talk to others who have worked with the mediator in the past to ensure his character is strong and his results are credible. Second, verify up front the fees or costs of the mediator's services so there are no surprise bills or sudden requests to split his commission.

44. No More Mr. Nice Guy

This tactic is particularly effective when your counterpart is not being honest or is pushing you to the end of your rope with excessive demands. You take something back that you have already agreed to earlier in the negotiation.

EXAMPLE

Lloyd and Nancy have been renting an apartment from the same landlord for three years. For about six months, they have been feeling ill and going to the doctor repeatedly, but no one can figure out what their problem is. One day, while moving furniture, they find an entire wall covered with black mold. After doing some research, they discover that this mold could very well be what has been causing their health problems. On March 10, Lloyd and

Nancy move out of the apartment and send the landlord a notice that they will not return until the moldy wall has been repaired. By March 20, the landlord has taken no action, so the next day Lloyd and Nancy send a letter stating that they are permanently moving out and requesting that the landlord refund their deposit. This seems to them like a fair request. When the landlord refuses to return the deposit, saying that Lloyd and Nancy have not provided thirty days' notice, they hire an attorney, who sends another letter demanding that the couple's deposit be returned, and that the rent for March be refunded as well.

COUNTER

A fair and honest person would probably have quickly repaired the moldy wall or returned the security deposit as requested, and therefore would not need any counter to this tactic. However, looking at the negotiation from the landlord's point of view, he could try asking if the couple would be satisfied if he fulfilled the original request for a repair. Another option would be to show how he has been working on solving Lloyd and Nancy's problem, using *Facts and Statistics* (he has been collecting bids for the repair, etc.). Or he can agree to the lawyer's demands but try to gain something in return, using the *Trade-off Concession* tactic: "I will agree to cut a check right now for the entire month's rent and the security deposit if you will sign an agreement not to hold me liable for any future concerns related to the moldy wall."

45. Persistence

If you have children, especially teenagers, you know that sometimes you may give in to their demands just to be able to get on with your life. The same tactic works quite well in the business world.

EXAMPLE

I have a son who is a master at asking for something over and over again, from many different creative angles, until he accomplishes his goal. At one time, his major life goal was to own the latest version of PlayStation. He asked for one almost every day for a period of a year. His creative questions included "Could I buy it with my own money?" He also asked why other parents I respect bought *their* kids a PlayStation. The questions went on and on. I even told him, "PlayStation is a dead horse in our house, and if the horse is dead, you should get off it!" Refusing to give up, my son creatively asked the following great question: "Dad, is it important to you and Mom that I can make quick decisions in complex situations?" When I said "yes," he came back with "Great! I think the newest version of PlayStation helps kids make quick decisions in complex situations." After one year, he finally got his PlayStation. As I read this account, I understand why persistence is such a successful tactic.

COUNTER

In this particular example, my best defense would probably have been a solid track record of not caving in to persistence. A second effective tactic would have been *No More Mr. Nice Guy*—I could have removed a deal point that my son felt had already been conceded. For example, I could have said, "If you bring up PlayStation one more time this week, I will take away your Netflix privileges for the rest of the week." Since movies are as high on this boy's "explicit need" list as PlayStation, this tactic might have worked well.

46. Electronic Shark in the Moat

To be an effective negotiator, you need access to the person who has the knowledge and ability to negotiate. Many years ago, secretaries played the role of "shark in the moat," letting only a few select people have contact with their bosses. Today we are technologically advanced—we have *Electronic Sharks in the Moat* (voice mail, email, text). It's difficult to negotiate when you can't get past a person's electronic shark. Some negotiators use this tactic to their advantage, stalling a negotiation by creating the perception that they are too busy to respond to a counterpart's request.

EXAMPLE

A commercial real estate professional is trying to secure an appointment with a corporate executive. No matter how many times the real estate professional makes contact, he constantly reaches the executive's email or voicemail, and the executive herself or her assistant calls back at odd hours and leaves a voicemail or an email in response. Although the responses give the real estate professional hope of an eventual meeting, the *Electronic Shark in the Moat* is very effective at keeping a distance between the two counterparts.

COUNTER

The real estate professional could try calling very early in the morning or very late in the afternoon, when there is less chance that the *Electronic Shark in the Moat* is on duty. A second tactic is to utilize *Find Us an Umpire* (either within or outside the executive's company) to help bring the two people together.

47. Stalling for Concessions

Salespeople are typically short on patience when they smell a deal in the air. In fact, sales trainers sometimes teach that if you do not strike while the iron is hot, you might lose the deal. But impatience often encourages negotiators to make concessions that may not be necessary. Knowing this, a savvy counterpart might stall for time, trying to make you nervous and more willing to make trade-offs.

EXAMPLE

A saleswoman prepares a proposal for a customer and, over the next few days, calls or emails two or three times to ask what the customer thinks of the proposal. The customer never responds because he is stalling, hoping the saleswoman will be willing to make some concessions if she feels he isn't particularly interested in making a deal. Worried that the customer might be doing business with a competitor, the saleswoman gets nervous. Although she is not sure if the customer has even had time to review any of her proposals, the saleswoman leaves a message that her "numbers are ballpark, based on the information given, and there is room to negotiate."

COUNTER

You should never discount a price before your counterpart tells you there is a need to do so. The best counter in this situation would probably be for the saleswoman to wait patiently for a reply. Or she could write a letter to the customer, stating, "I have tried to get in contact with you several times over the last week, and for whatever reason, we have been unable to connect." Under no circumstances should she leave any more phone or email messages.

When a counterpart is obviously stalling, be patient. Don't keep using the same tactic to make contact. Think like a dolphin and do something different.

48. Massaging a Big Ego

Asking a question like "Do you have the power to make this deal happen?" can be an effective tactic. Some people feel compelled to say "yes" for the sole reason that it strokes their ego. People with big egos believe they are always right, and like to feel in charge.

EXAMPLE

A man goes out to buy a car for his family. He is a bottom-line, results-oriented type of guy who is good at negotiating a great deal. Once he makes the decision to buy a car, he wants to go out, do the research, take a test drive, negotiate a deal, and purchase the car all in one afternoon. The salesperson, sensing the buyer's need for power, asks, "Will you be making this decision without your wife?" The husband replies, "I am the sole decision maker when it comes to purchasing the family car."

COUNTER

Obviously, the tactic of *Higher Authority* would work best here—and it is probably in this man's best interest to employ it. He could say, "Although my wife and I usually agree on this type of purchase, I will have to review the purchase agreement with her to gain her approval."

It is usually wise to get someone else to review any deal you are structuring. Asking someone else to review your proposed outcome is not a sign of weakness, but a sign of strength.

49. Losing the Battle to Win the War

To promote the long-term best interests of a relationship or accomplish a larger goal, conceding a deal point may sometimes be the best option.

EXAMPLE

A woman wants to purchase a brand-new home that is going to cost almost $150,000 more than the home she and her husband are currently living in. Taking on that much new debt scares her husband. He tells his wife that the new home is a huge financial stretch for them and he does not think they should buy it at this time. The wife responds by saying she would consider staying in the current home if they could get new carpet and have the kitchen remodeled. Knowing that these changes will cost a lot less than the debt on a new home, the husband agrees to the carpet and remodel.

COUNTER

The wife has already countered in this negotiation by presenting the remodel as an alternative to purchasing a new home. To maintain a healthy relationship with her husband, she might want to accept this win-win outcome.

50. Power of Competition

In most businesses, the *Power of Competition* can be devastating. The seller who knows that a customer can easily go to the competition for the same product or service has to justify everything and may end up giving away more than originally planned. Sometimes, just the threat of competition is enough to force concessions.

EXAMPLE

Using the *Power of Competition,* a client states, "I have gotten three bids, and yours is five hundred dollars higher than the other two. I would really like to work with you, but your price is too high."

COUNTER

To counter this challenge, the vendor should defend her price, citing her product's quality and service. Once we were out on a sales call with a seasoned veteran who responded to a client's question about price by stating matter-of-factly, "Mrs. Jones, my price is higher than the competition's because I am the one who is going to do the job right." He said this so confidently that he convinced the client *and* us.

Realize that many clients will say your price is too high just to get rid of you when they have no intention of working with you even if you do lower your price.

51. Putting It in Writing

Whenever you and a counterpart reach agreement in a negotiation, you should be the one to put the agreement in writing. This gives you the opportunity to tie down any loose ends.

EXAMPLE

You agree to lease 4,000 square feet of office space for $4,000 per month. As part of the deal, you agree to sign a two-year lease, and the building owner agrees to give you one month's free rent. After the handshake, you offer to put the terms in writing. Tying down the loose ends in your favor, you write:

- Two-year lease commencing September 1
- Price of $4,000 per month for 4,000 square feet, on a gross basis, not triple net *(The difference between these small words can add up to hundreds of dollars each month. On a gross rent, the landlord pays all extra costs, such as taxes, garbage removal, cleaning fees, etc.)*
- Free rent for one month beginning with the September 1 move-in date *(Some landlords like to put the free rent in the middle or at the end of the lease.)*

COUNTER

If the landlord does not agree with how you have tied up the loose ends in your written agreement, he should immediately fax or write to you, explaining how he thinks the issues should be handled. If he does not respond immediately, he will lose tremendous bargaining power when the two of you reconvene at the negotiating table.

52. Feel, Felt, and Found

Feel, Felt, and Found is effective for helping your counterpart understand your point of view.

EXAMPLE

The buyer states, "I can't believe you're asking thirty thousand dollars for this software package." The seller responds, "I can understand how you *feel* about the price. Many other owners have *felt* the same way until they *found* out how trouble-free and long-lasting our software is. There really is a difference, and that is what makes this price such a great value."

COUNTER

The buyer could respond with *That's Not Good Enough,* insisting that $30,000 is simply too much, then pausing and waiting for the seller's response. Or the buyer could appeal to a *Higher Authority,* explaining that his wife, boss, or business partner will let him spend only $25,000. Finally, he could use the tactic of the *Trade-off Concession* and agree to pay the $30,000 if the seller will throw in service and support for one year.

53. These Boots Are Made for Walking

In any relationship, the side with the least commitment to continuing the relationship has the most power. Being able to walk away from the bargaining table when the tide turns against you gives you leverage.

EXAMPLE

Kathleen wants to buy a desk for her daughter. The desk has been advertised for $277. When Kathleen starts to pay for the desk, the salesman tells her there is an additional $85 fee for assembling the desk. Kathleen doesn't want to pay the fee, since she and her husband can assemble the desk. The salesman writes up the contract without including the assembly charge.

A week later, when Kathleen and her husband go to pick up the desk, the clerk behind the counter states that there must have been a mistake made because the desk is already assembled and you need to pay the additional $85 fee. At that point, Kathleen says, "Just give me my $277 back and we'll buy the desk somewhere else."

COUNTER

If someone uses *These Boots Are Made for Walking* on you and you can meet your goals without that person (e.g., other people are interested in your product or service), let your counterpart walk. In the example above, the clerk apparently thinks the store can sell the desk to someone else for the full price plus the charge for assembling the desk, so he is not concerned that Kathleen is walking away. If he decides that waiving the $85 charge is a small concession to make, he may utilize the tactic of *Losing the Battle to Win the War*. But if the clerk ends up chasing after Kathleen and bringing her back to the bargaining table, his power will deteriorate considerably. Car salespeople are notorious for going after customers when they start to walk away. Remember, if you keep walking, the leverage will be on your side, as long as you have a way of contacting your counterpart again should you desire.

54. Conditional No

This tactic is designed for all the really nice people of the world who find it just too difficult to look their counterparts in the eyes and say, "No, I am not going to do that!"

EXAMPLE

You have a coworker who asks you if you would work late in her place on Friday evening, closing the office. You agree. The following Friday, she asks you the same thing, saying that she is having babysitting challenges and needs to leave early. Being a mom yourself, you understand childcare problems. Since you think it important to support team members, you agree to help her out one more time. However, the third Friday that she asks you to cover for her, you respond with a *Conditional No*. You tell her that under normal circumstances, you'd be happy to help out. However, this Friday you need pick up your own children and must leave the office by 5 p.m. You let her know that next month, you'd be happy to help her out again.

COUNTER

The easiest counter would be for the coworker to thank the coworker for standing in for her for the past two weeks and then find someone else to work late.

55. Building a Bridge

Sometimes you need to toss your counterpart a rope or build a bridge that provides a path to a win-win negotiation.

EXAMPLE

A business owner is trying to get a major corporation as a customer. After a year of effort, the corporation has still not even given the vendor a project to bid on. So the owner of the business calls the corporate buyer with a proposition: "I want so much to work with your corporation," he says, "that I am willing to do the first job, up to five hundred dollars for free. With no money at risk, would you be willing to let me do one job so we can demonstrate our quality and service?" The corporate buyer agrees.

COUNTER

If the corporate buyer does not want to switch vendors, the best counter in this situation would be a simple refusal of the offer. The corporate buyer could also use a *Conditional No,* saying that he is unable to give the owner a job right now but may have a project for him in the next month.

56. The Puppy Dog

The power behind *The Puppy Dog* tactic lies in letting your counterpart have the object she is negotiating for before the deal is finalized. The name is derived from the tactic pet store owners use when they tell you to go ahead and hold the puppies and play with them while you consider buying one. I once ended up with a $1,400 Old English sheepdog because of this very tactic. With Sir Bentley licking me on the face, $1,400 seemed quite reasonable!

EXAMPLE

Michael wants to buy a used boat but he and the owner are stuck on the price. The owner suggests that Michael take the boat to a nearby island for the weekend. The owner is convinced that at the end of the weekend, Michael will feel the boat is worth the full asking price. When Michael returns from a great weekend, he continues to try to get the owner to sell the boat for a lower price. But the owner says he is confident he can find another buyer who will pay the full price. The owner is a smart man. He knows that after a great weekend, Michael has already bought the boat in his mind. In fact, he would probably be willing to pay even more money if the owner raised the price.

COUNTER

The tactic of *The Puppy Dog* is so powerful that the only effective counter is *These Boots Are Made for Walking*. If Michael wants to continue negotiating the price, he should remove himself from the picture and let a third party negotiate for him. Once his emotions have been committed and the boat owner knows it, Michael is in a very vulnerable position.

57. The Ball Is in Your Court

This tactic is effective for determining what creative options your counterpart can come up with to help you achieve your goal. You present a challenge that your counterpart needs to help you overcome if the negotiation is to be completed.

EXAMPLE

An insurance company's office supply manager tells a vendor, "I really enjoy working with you and I think your equipment and service are exactly what we need. The problem is, we have a budget of only $150,000 and you have quoted nearly $165,000. What can you do to help us stay within the budget?"

COUNTER

There are at least four possible counters to this tactic: (1) The vendor could explain how his products and services are designed to improve the insurance company's long-term bottom line (e.g., by minimizing repairs or lengthening the time before a replacement is needed). (2) The vendor could use the *Feel, Felt, and Found* tactic, stating, "I understand you *feel* our price is a little high. Other customers have *felt* the same way at first but have *found* after a few years that our product and service are the best values on the market." (3) Appealing to a *Higher Authority* might also be effective. The vendor could ask, "Could you check with your manager to see if the budget can be revised?" (4) Last, the vendor could try the *If . . . Then* tactic: "If we substituted a one-year warranty for our usual three-year warranty, then we could come a lot closer to your budgeted number. Would that be of interest to you?" The *If . . . Then* tactic usually leads to further negotiation and increases the probability of a win-win outcome for both counterparts.

58. Give It to Me Straight

Before you make concessions based on what a counterpart tells you, it is good practice to verify anything you are not sure about.

EXAMPLE

You are purchasing a new phone, and the saleswoman is trying to sell you insurance, since this would mean an additional commission for her. She tells you that the insurance covers everything, including water damage, drops, broken screen, etc. You ask to see the details on the insurance policy. After reading the section on coverage, you point out that a broken screen would be covered only if you paid an additional hundred dollars on top of the monthly insurance premium. Taking the time to verify facts will make you a better negotiator.

COUNTER

There really is no good counter for the saleswoman once her "facts" are proven wrong or she is perceived to have omitted important information in an attempt to sell the insurance. That is why it is best for negotiators to be honest and forthright and make sure they always have their facts straight. If they are not sure about something, they should simply say so. A negotiator whose facts and figures are proved wrong will lose credibility and leverage in the relationship.

59. The Threat

The Threat is one of the most pervasive tactics utilized by counterparts who cannot achieve their goals or resolve their differences through normal one-on-one communication.

EXAMPLE

A manager suspends an employee for one week for insubordination. The employee responds, "You had better think twice about what you are doing to me. When I leave here, I'm going call my attorney."

COUNTER

The manager, in consultation with his human resources partner, might ask questions to gain information that clarifies exactly why the employee feels the need to contact a lawyer. For example, the manager might respond, "Of course, you have the right to contact an attorney. How will that help you in your current situation?" A second effective counter would be the tactic of *Focusing on the Future*. The manager might ask, "What do you feel we could do differently next week so we don't encounter this problem again?"

Note that we are not saying that employees should not utilize the law to rectify wrongs when management has dealt unjustly with them. What we are saying is that these tactics take time and money. We are also saying that when the goal is to build long-term win-win relationships, resolving a negotiation without beginning a lawsuit or filing a grievance is better—*if* the issues can be satisfactorily resolved without these alternatives.

60. Investing Time

Getting a counterpart to invest time in a negotiation gives you leverage. The more time people put into any endeavor, the more committed they become to the outcome, even when the outcome is not in their best interests.

EXAMPLE

I recently bought a new camera. I had spent about two hours at the store listening to the options and benefits of the various cameras being sold and was ready to buy. But when the store clerk was entering the sale into the computer, she discovered that the desired model was no longer in stock. Rather than starting all over again, I quickly made a second choice. After two hours, there was no way I was going home without a new camera!

COUNTER

Several possible counters were available to me. Utilizing *Asking a Closed-Ended Question,* I could have asked, "When will the camera be in stock?" or "Which of your other stores currently has this camera available?" Or I could have suggested that the clerk *Sweeten the Deal,* and said, "I will go ahead and buy this other camera that I do not like as much if you will throw in a camera bag and a memory card for my inconvenience."

61. Appealing to St. Teresa

Looking your counterpart in the eye and saying, "I have a problem and I need your help," can be very effective. Why? Because this tactic touches the part of human nature that wants to be strong and help others. You are asking your counterpart to be as noble and giving as St. Teresa. Only a very cold person finds it easy to respond, "I can't help you."

EXAMPLE

An employee walks into his boss's office and admits, "I have some problems and I need your help. I have recently gone through a divorce, my rent has just increased, and my oldest child is now going to college. I really like working for you and this company. Is there anything you can do to help me earn a higher income here so I don't need to go looking for a higher-paying job?"

COUNTER

Of course, the manager could simply say no. Another option would be to issue a *Conditional No,* stating, "I cannot give you a raise today, but I will consider it in three months when we start the next fiscal year." Third, utilizing *There Is More Than One Way to Cook an Egg,* the manager might suggest, "Although I cannot give you a raise in your current position, we could talk about other positions in the company that pay more money." Fourth, the manager may want to say, *"I'll Think About It and Get Back to You Later"* to buy some time. No matter which counter the manager chooses, he should empathize with the employee, who is in a difficult situation.

62. Help Me Understand

Some authors on negotiation encourage readers to ask only questions to which they already know the answers. Although we agree that you may not want to ask questions in some situations, we support asking questions when you don't understand your counterpart's position. Asking for clarification or more information from your counterpart can be very helpful in creating a win-win outcome.

EXAMPLE

An Internet provider offers their most attractive rate, but only when a customer signs up for e-billing. While most customers seem to like being able to pay their bills electronically, many still complain about not being able to get a hard copy of their bills in the mail or being able to pay by check. The Internet provider justifies its decision about not mailing billing notices or accepting checks by educating customers about the cost savings, which are being passed on to the customer.

COUNTER

In this situation, the customer can employ two tactics: the tactic of *Higher Authority* and the tactic of *If . . . Then*. The customer asks to speak to the employee's manager and asks, "If I mail my payment five days before the due date, will you accept my check and send me a statement each month?

63. Playing Stupid

Playing Stupid sometimes pays off. You may ask a question even when you already know the answer, in order to verify the accuracy of your counterpart's information and/or test his honesty. This tactic works because people tend to want to help you more when they think you are handicapped by a lack of skills, knowledge, or information. In other words, there are times when playing dumb is smart.

EXAMPLE

Last year we were in the market for a new refrigerator for our office. Wanting to make a good investment, we researched several different brands of refrigerators we thought would work and then shopped three big appliance suppliers. After our in-store visits, we began to realize that we knew more about the models than the salespeople waiting on us. But because too much knowledge would probably intimidate the salespeople and cause them to keep their guard up, we began *Playing Stupid,* explaining that we were a bit overwhelmed with all the options available.

Finally, when the fourth salesperson had concluded his presentation, we narrowed the focus to the model we were interested in and told the salesperson that if he could sell us that refrigerator for $1,200, we would make the purchase right then and there, without even checking the price at other stores. This was $99 off his asking price and $135 off the lowest price we had found at the other stores.

COUNTER

In the scenario above, the salesman responded, "I can't give this refrigerator to you for $1,200, but I can let you have it for $1,250." It was still a great deal, so we agreed. Remember to keep your guard up in every negotiation. Realize that any information you yield may be used against you. Helping a stupid person is a good thing, but it is devastating to help a smart person dig a grave for you!

64. Fait Accompli—Asking for Forgiveness

Fait Accompli is a tactic described by Gerard I. Nierenberg. The phrase is French for "accomplished fact," and refers to a deed that is already done—and is therefore irreversible. You employ this tactic when you do something without first negotiating it. Then, when you get caught, you respond to any questions with something like "Who, me? I didn't know I wasn't supposed to be doing that. I apologize. I will not do it anymore."

EXAMPLE

Your neighbors' trees are hanging over your property and you are tired of raking up the leaves. Instead of making a big deal and asking your neighbors to cut the trees back to the property line, you decide to trim them yourself. Your neighbors become incensed that you have cut their trees without asking. You reply simply that you thought you were doing the right thing by not bothering them, and you apologize for your actions.

COUNTER

The reason this tactic is so powerful is that there are few tactics to counter it. What is done, is done. About the only thing the neighbors can do is stop future progress. For example, if you are still cutting the trees, the neighbors could ask you to stop, saying they will hire a professional to trim their own trees. Putting the process on hold puts them in a better position to enforce future action. They could also use the *Safeguard* tactic to guide the future relationship, asking you to agree that you will never cut the trees again without first getting their permission.

65. Taking a Time-out

Taking a break from a negotiation can sometimes be the best thing for both counterparts. You may just want to get something to eat or drink, let tension disperse, or locate additional information before making a decision. A break might last ten minutes, overnight, or a whole weekend. Novice negotiators have to learn to feel comfortable saying, "Let's take a break."

EXAMPLE

All parents have a difficult discussion or two with their children at some point. The topic of the discussion may be school grades, curfew, telling the truth, or enforcing discipline. Sometimes a discussion does not go well. The parents end up angry, raising their voices and saying things they regret later. The child ends up frustrated and in tears. At a time like this, a great question for parents to ask themselves is "If we get angry enough to say things we might later regret and our child ends up in tears, will we have accomplished our goal?" If the answer is no, it may be time to take a break.

COUNTER

If your child thinks he is "winning" the discussion and you are taking a break for the sole purpose of avoiding the issue being discussed, he may want to insist on resolving the issue immediately. As another option, he could make sure you establish a specific time to reconvene.

66. Two Heads Are Better Than One

Although it is always good to have a plan complete with solutions laid out in your mind, getting your counterpart involved in generating win-win solutions can also be helpful. Your counterpart may well suggest an idea you had not considered.

EXAMPLE

A client informs a consulting firm that she is having major customer service complaints and feels her staff needs training. While the consultant has a good idea about the type of employee and management training the company needs, instead of making suggestions, the consultant asks, "What type of training do you feel would work best for your managers and employees?" Clients usually have a very good idea of the prescription needed to cure their problems.

COUNTER

A counter will probably not be necessary with this tactic. But the client could employ the tactic of *Deflecting an Answer with a Great Question* to change the course of the conversation, if desired. She might also try *Sharing Both Pros and Cons* of various possible solutions.

67. Salami

Few people eat a whole salami with one swallow. Salami just goes down easier if you cut it into small pieces. The same principle applies to negotiation. Your counterpart will be more likely to make major concessions with less resistance if you cut the concessions into several small pieces.

EXAMPLE

Kate is in the market for a new security system for her house. She has received three bids and the total system she wants retails for $1,850. She has set a goal of purchasing the system for $1,500. If she walks right up to a salesman and says she will buy the system for $1,500, he will probably tell her to get lost. She stands a much higher chance of getting the system at her price if she uses the *Salami* tactic.

First, Kate asks the salesman what kind of discount he will give if she purchases all components at once, including remote monitoring capabilities. He might agree to a 10 percent discount. Next, she asks if he will take another $200 off if she agrees to a two-year monitoring contract. Finally, she mentions that she will buy the equipment immediately if the salesperson will throw in the remote monitoring video surveillance at no additional charge. Before you know it, all those little concessions add up to $350.

COUNTER

If the salesperson realizes he is getting the *Salami,* he has several options. He can expose Kate's technique, pointing out that he has made concession after concession, and the negotiation is no longer win-win. Second, he can blow up, using the *Wow! You've Got to Be Kidding!* tactic. When Kate asks for one more concession, he can express utter disbelief, acting as though she has finally introduced the straw that has broken the camel's back.

68. Referencing a Benchmark

Objective criteria are often useful as a baseline for negotiations. Some well-known standard benchmarks include the *Kelley Blue Book*, the Consumer Price Index, the Consumer Confidence Index, and the interest rate set by the Federal Reserve Bank.

Whenever someone buys or sells an automobile, for example, each counterpart has the opportunity to reference the *Kelley Blue Book* for objective criteria. This source provides the retail and wholesale value of the car and specifies how much various options are worth. It even tells how much money to deduct or add for specific mileage.

EXAMPLE

You are asking $17,500 for a car you are selling. A potential buyer tells you that according to the *Kelley Blue Book*, the value of your car is just $15,000.

COUNTER

When a counterpart *References a Benchmark*, you should first verify that his information is correct. There are lots of ways to present information, and your counterpart will probably present his statistics in a way that supports his position. For example, if he tells you the *Kelley Blue Book* values your car at $15,000, ask, "Are you referencing the dealer value or the private party value?" Buyers usually reference the dealer-valued estimate, which is lower. Or, are you referencing a car that is in excellent, fair, or poor condition?

A second tactic may be to provide new information from

another source, referencing Edmunds.com, which supports your price for this make and model car.

Finally, you might take a different angle and explain why your car is an exception to the objective criteria. Perhaps you have kept the car in perfect condition and have all the maintenance records to prove it, and you believe these exceptions support your price.

69. We've Never Done That Before

When you cite a precedent, you use something that has happened in the past to justify a current request, position, or concession. Lawyers often cite precedents, using actual court cases to support their positions. Reversing this tactic by saying "There is no precedent for that" or *"We've Never Done That Before"* in reference to a deal point can be very effective.

EXAMPLE

A hotel guest asks to extend his checkout until 2 p.m. The guest services person denies the request, saying, "I am sorry for any inconvenience, but we never extend checkouts past twelve noon."

COUNTER

The hotel guest could respond by *Asking a Closed-Ended Question,* such as "How much would it cost to stay an additional two hours?" Or he could counter with a precedent by pointing out, "Every time I have stayed with this hotel chain before, I have been allowed a two p.m. checkout when I requested it." As a last resort, he could utilize the tactic of the *Higher Authority,* going over the guest services person's head and asking to speak to the manager.

70. Apparent Withdrawal

Sometimes, although you may not want to go to the extreme of walking away from a deal, you do want to give your counterpart the feeling that you are not *really* committed. *Apparent Withdrawal* should be used when you want to give the appearance that you do not care, when in reality you are simply trying to retain control of the situation.

EXAMPLE

Several years ago, a friend of ours was negotiating to buy a beautiful home. He had gone through several days of negotiating on many deal points. He was in love with the house but the seller's last concession was still $14,000 above what our friend wanted to pay. He asked his real estate broker to let the seller's broker know that he was going to have to withdraw from buying the house because he could not make the numbers work to his satisfaction. Our friend was confident that neither the seller nor the broker would let a $550,000 deal go over a difference of $14,000. Since our friend was willing to pay the $14,000 if he had to, this was a case of *Apparent Withdrawal* rather than *Withdrawn Offer,* discussed below.

COUNTER

The broker had at least three possible tactics at her disposal: *These Boots Are Made for Walking, I'll Meet You in the Middle,* or *Trade-off Concession.* Any of these tactics could have worked to bring our friend back to the bargaining table without giving in to his lower price.

71. Withdrawn Offer

Actually withdrawing your initial offer may be in your best interest in some situations. This tactic can be used when you feel you are being taken advantage of or put in a position where you can only lose.

EXAMPLE

Joseph is selling a house that he owns jointly with a partner. The asking price is $326,000. The buyer is a very tough negotiator. By using the *Salami* tactic, he manages to reduce the price to $310,000, have the escrow extended to ninety days, and stipulate that Joseph and his partner fix any repairs noted in the inspection report. Joseph thinks the deal is finalized. Then the buyer brings his wife into the picture.

The buyer's wife says she hates the kitchen and will not allow her husband to pay any more than $300,000 for the house. That is when Joseph says he has bad news for the buyer: Joseph's partner has decided that they should not sell the house for any less than $315,000. Since the buyer really does want the house, he spends the rest of his negotiating energy trying to get the price back down to $310,000.

COUNTER

First, rather than scrambling to get the price back down, the buyer could utilize *These Boots Are Made for Walking*. If Joseph really wants to make the deal, he will come back. Second, the buyer could use *Apparent Withdrawal*, giving the appearance that he is quitting, to regain control of the situation.

72. Low- or Highballing

In *Low- or Highballing,* someone makes a ridiculously low or high offer.

EXAMPLE

You are trying to sell your house for $289,000. Your agent brings you an offer of $260,000 from a couple who saw the house over the weekend. If your house is competitively priced, this would be considered a lowball offer.

Lowballing is effective because it tends to lower a counterpart's aspirations. If you counter the couple's offer with $280,000, their next offer of $275,000 will not seem so bad. If they had originally offered you $275,000, you would probably have countered higher than $280,000.

EXAMPLE

If someone lowballs you, you have three options: (1) Do not counter! Utilize *These Boots Are Made for Walking* and move on. (2) Counter by repeating your asking price. (3) Using the tactic of the *Withdrawn Offer,* counter with a figure higher than your asking price. Explain that the couple must have misunderstood the actual price, and then counter their ridiculous offer with an even more ridiculous price.

If someone highballs you, you also have three options: (1) Do your homework to find out whether the price is competitive. (2) Use the *Power of Competition.* Demonstrate with a competitive analysis that the price is unreasonably high. (3) Ask for a price breakdown.

73. Funny Money

With this tactic, you break dollars and cents down into such small amounts that your counterpart doesn't realize he is dealing with large sums of money.

EXAMPLE

Several times a month, there's a knock at our door from a representative of a solar company installing solar panels at a home nearby. Because they are already in the neighborhood, they can offer us substantial savings on installing a solar system to get us "off the grid." They present a persuasive argument, saying that solar is "cool" for many reasons. They then ask how much we are currently paying for electricity. Once they know that amount, they are quickly able to project how much money we'd save in a ten-year period by switching to solar, saying that with that amount saved, we could easily afford to buy a new car or take a luxury trip. Finally, they tell us that by using solar, we will only be spending less than eight cents a day for electricity. Who would not want to spend just eight cents a day to help save money and be environmentally conscious? While the eight cents a day is accurate, what they don't make really clear is that you will be spending more than ten *dollars* a day for the next ten years to pay off the financing on your solar investment. The funny money, just eight cents a day, can be very persuasive if you don't project out the cost of the solar installation.

Car dealerships are masters of the *Funny Money* tactic. They try to get the buyer to think only about the monthly payment and keep him in the dark about the total price and interest rate until the deal has been struck.

COUNTER

In both examples above, the buyers should do their homework and spend some time working out the total price. If their counterparts are unwilling to provide a full disclosure of all terms, the buyers should simply walk away from the deal.

74. The False Alarm (Did I Forget to Tell You About . . . ?)

Have you ever been involved in a negotiation and thought you had concluded a deal, only to learn that the other person was just getting started? This is known as *The False Alarm*.

EXAMPLE

You are buying a commercial building. You negotiate with the owner and agree on a price of $940,000. You are convinced you have a deal. Later that day, the owner of the building calls to tell you he has presented the offer to his business partner, and his partner reminded him that although the sale price of $940,000 was accurate, he had forgotten that there would be an additional $6,500 in loan payoffs on the property that he expected us to pay.

COUNTER

There are several possible counters. First, when the owner tells you about his partner's increase in price, you could use the tactic of the *Withdrawn Offer*. Tell him you shared the deal with *your* business partner and she will not let you pay more than $935,000.

(This also employs the tactic of the *Higher Authority*.) Second, you could expose the owner's tactic and say that the deal you struck is good only for twenty-four hours. If he does not take the deal right away, you will have to start the negotiations over again. Third, you could employ *These Boots Are Made for Walking*. Finally, you could utilize the *Trade-off Concession*, saying, "Yes, I will pay $940,000 plus the additional loan charges, but only if you paint and recarpet the entire building."

75. The Choice Is Yours

You can use this tactic when you have several alternatives that are acceptable to you. Salespeople are trained to use this approach to gain a buyer's commitment.

EXAMPLE

A car buyer tells the salesman, "I am willing to buy your new Chevy Silverado pickup for $29,195 at three percent interest. However, if you want me to pay five percent interest you have offered, you will have to throw in the paint sealant, bed liner, upgraded navigation system, and floor mats. Either way. *The Choice Is Yours.*"

COUNTER

The salesman has lots of options here, including: (1) saying no to both deals and starting over; (2) making a counteroffer to one deal or the other; (3) using *Apparent Withdrawal;* (4) employing *These Boots Are Made for Walking;* or (5) making a *Trade-off Concession.*

76. Never Saying Yes to the First Offer

Have you ever felt that you paid too much for something? Chances are you felt that way because you did not have to fight hard enough for your outcome. When someone says yes to your first offer, you walk away with one of two feelings: You may think you paid too much, or, as if that feeling were not enough to make you have buyer's remorse, you may think something is wrong with what you just bought!

EXAMPLE

A woman is buying a used couch at a garage sale. She challenges the seller with, "You are asking six hundred dollars for this couch. Would you consider taking five hundred?" The seller responds, "Sure, five hundred dollars. It's a deal!"

COUNTER

First, this is the time to use the tactic of *The False Alarm*. The buyer could say she was just asking if $500 would be acceptable, but she thinks that is still too much to pay. Then she could raise her level of aspiration. Second, she could use the *Higher Authority* tactic, telling the seller that $500 sounds reasonable to her, but she needs her husband to come over and take a look at the couch.

77. The Decoy

With *The Decoy,* you make a big issue of something you don't care much about when you are really after something else more important to you.

EXAMPLE

You are buying a new copier and you strike a deal. The only option the copier does not have is Bluetooth connectivity, which the dealer agrees to install for you. When you are getting ready to sign the papers, the dealer informs you that it will take a month to get the copier ready and the Bluetooth feature installed. Although the time frame is not that important to you, you make a big issue of it, hoping that the dealer will make another price concession. In fact, you even tell the dealer you will go somewhere else if he cannot make the long wait worth your while.

COUNTER

If he suspects your motives, the dealer can utilize *Uncovering the Real Reason* to expose your tactic. Other options are *Apparent Withdrawal* and *These Boots Are Made for Walking*.

78. The Dead Fish

You place a deal point on the bargaining table that you do not expect to achieve and do not particularly care about, knowing that it will be about as acceptable to your counterpart as the smell of a dead fish. When your counterpart makes a stink, you offer to give up the deal point, but you make it sound like a big concession on your part so you can ask for something in return.

EXAMPLE

Consuela is buying a used car from Josh. Josh is asking $10,000. Consuela wants to pay less, so she lays *The Dead Fish* on the table, asking Josh to purchase new tires. She lets Josh know that she is willing to drop the new tires demand, but only if he lowers his price by $400.

COUNTER

Josh could simply insist that the price is not negotiable. Or he could use *Apparent Withdrawal, These Boots Are Made for Walking,* or the *Trade-off Concession.*

79. Standard Practice or Policy

Standard Practice or Policy is a tactic used to convince a counterpart to proceed in a certain way simply because that way is "policy." This tactic works well because it suggests that the way being proposed is the usual or customary procedure and, therefore, is probably the safest approach.

The most common example is the standard contract. The party being asked to sign a standard contract will probably just assume that the contract does not need to be changed. However, questioning just how "standard" a contract really is usually produces good results.

EXAMPLE

Fernando is renting some office space. The landlord hands Fernando a lease to sign, saying, "It's a standard commercial lease. Just initial it in two places and sign at the bottom."

COUNTER

Fernando has several options here. Using the tactic of the *Salami*, he could start slicing away, ever so slightly, at what is considered "standard," agreeing to some terms of the lease but not others. He could use the tactic of the *Trade-off Concession,* agreeing to all the terms of the lease in return for one month's free rent. He could rewrite the contract to suit his own needs. Or, utilizing the tactic of *These Boots Are Made for Walking,* he could always leave and go rent space from someone else.

80. Reward in Heaven

One counterpart in a negotiation may promise the other counterpart, "If you can meet my demands, I will reward you at a later date."

EXAMPLE

I once negotiated with an experienced procurement manager. When I was reviewing the project he wanted me to give him a quote on, he made a point of telling me how much future work he was going to be purchasing down the road. Naturally, when I quoted the job, I gave him a very low price because I wanted his future business. When I called the buyer back with the quote, he said that he really wanted to use me but my price was higher than he had expected. He offered, "If you can reduce the price another five thousand dollars on this project, I will give you all my future work." In effect, he was promising that I would get my *Reward in Heaven.*

COUNTER

Unfortunately, most people fall for this tactic. My experience has taught me that the promised reward rarely comes through.

One possible response is to simply fight fire with fire. Using the tactic of the *Trade-off Concession,* I might say, "I am not able to discount this job, but if you give me this job and then have another one for me in the next thirty days, I will discount the second job." A second effective counter could be citing *Standard Practice or Policy:* "It is not my company's policy to discount first-time jobs or allow me to discount a job on the promise of future business."

Experienced negotiators have been burned by this technique too often. Please spare yourself the frustration of not getting the reward!

81. The Power of Crazy

Once in a while, it pays to do something crazy—something so irrational that your counterpart will concede just to get rid of you. To make this technique effective, you have to do something so far afield from rational behavior that your actions are obviously absurd.

EXAMPLE

At the Department of Motor Vehicles, we once observed a woman who was so upset about having waited in three different lines without finding anyone who could solve her problem that she began crying and screaming, "All I want is for someone to treat me like a human being!" When this outburst started, a manager took the woman aside and personally helped her sort out her registration problems.

COUNTER

If someone uses this tactic on you, don't take the behavior personally. Realize that many negotiators do the absurd just for effect. You can always walk away until your counterpart agrees to become reasonable. Another possible tactic is *No More Mr. Nice Guy*. If your counterpart realizes that every time she becomes unreasonable, you withdraw the last offer you already agreed to, she will soon recognize that her behavior is costing her.

Another option is to get closer to someone who is acting crazy. Telling a person who is being absurd, "I love working with you because you display such great passion and emotion," usually diffuses the effectiveness of the crazy behavior.

82. How Would You Like to Pay for That?

With this tactic, you make an offer and assume that your counterpart will take it. You've undoubtedly met salespeople who, before a negotiation has been settled, just assume you will buy their product and ask, *"How Would You Like to Pay for That*—cash, credit card, or in-house financing?"

EXAMPLE

You are asking $300,000 for your house. You have stated that you will consider taking less if the buyer will agree to a short escrow, but you haven't specified how much less would be acceptable to you. The buyer says he will buy your house for $270,000 and asks if you would prefer a fifteen- or thirty-day escrow.

COUNTER

First, you could use the tactic of *Wow! You've Got to Be Kidding,* blowing up to get the price back to a respectable figure. Second, you could try making a *Trade-off Concession.* You could say that you will accept the price of $270,000 if the buyer will pay in cash and by the next day. Third, using *I'll Meet You in the Middle,* you could come up with a higher price and split the difference. Fourth, you could utilize *These Boots Are Made for Walking.*

83. Providing Negative Information

Sometimes you can change the power and direction of a negotiation simply by *Providing Negative Information.*

EXAMPLE

A saleswoman is making a product presentation to a customer, who eventually says he is thinking about buying the product from ABC Company, one of the saleswoman's competitors. The saleswoman knows that the recent issue of *Consumer Reports* contains an article that has a great deal of negative information about ABC's service, financial stability, and product quality. So she tells the customer, "Before you make a final decision, I recommend that you read the January issue of *Consumer Reports.* It has an article about ABC Company."

COUNTER

The customer has to do his homework and verify everything the salesperson says. The salesperson will undoubtedly weight the negative information about the competitor's product to be favorable to her own company. The customer should ask the saleswoman to explain why her product is superior to the competitor's, and substantiate her claims. If the customer is really interested in the competitor's product, he should provide the competitor with the opportunity to answer the negative claims made by both the saleswoman and *Consumer Reports*.

84. The Perfect Solution

When your counterpart lays a proposal, solution, or deal point on the table, it is a good idea to test how strongly that counterpart feels about his position. One great way to do this is to offer your counterpart *The Perfect Solution*.

EXAMPLE

A general contractor provides a proposal to build a patio and barbecue for a homeowner for $15,000. When the contractor states the price, the homeowner responds that he does not want to spend any more than $12,000. The contractor replies, "If I could design and build for you *The Perfect Solution* that meets all your patio and barbecue needs, would you be able to come up with the additional three thousand dollars?"

COUNTER

The homeowner could counter with the tactic of the *Higher Authority,* blaming the budget on his wife, their home equity line of credit, or someone or something else with decision-making power. Second, he could utilize the tactic of *Asking an Open-Ended Question* and ask the contractor, "If I cannot find an additional three thousand, what would you recommend I do?" Third, he might try the *Reward in Heaven* tactic, suggesting, "If you could build the patio and barbecue for close to twelve thousand, I will be a great reference for you for years to come." Fourth, he could ask the contractor for a breakdown of the costs to see if there are any parts of the project he could do himself.

85. You'll Be Sorry

When both sides in a negotiation have a great deal to lose if the negotiation fails and a great deal to win if it succeeds, the *You'll Be Sorry* tactic can be useful. One counterpart pushes the other right up to the edge of some terrible outcome, then threatens a final shove.

EXAMPLE

Negotiations between a home buyer and seller had gone several rounds. The price was agreed to and the property was in escrow. During escrow, the home repairs inspection was completed. Although none of the repairs were significant, the report showed the tile roof to be twenty years old. Even though there were no leaks or visible signs of wear or damage, the report indicated the property needed a new roof. The buyer countered by reducing the agreed upon price by $10,000 and stated they would walk away unless the price was reduced.

EXAMPLE

If a counterpart uses *You'll Be Sorry* against you and you believe that your counterpart has the power to back up the threat, you have two choices: you can utilize *These Boots Are Made for Walking* and accept the consequences, or you can decide what is most important to you and use the *Trade-off Concession* to negotiate other deal points.

86. Flattery or Sweet Talk

One effective way to gain leverage in a negotiation is to use *Flattery or Sweet Talk*. Used effectively, flattery has the impact of motivating the counterpart to respond.

EXAMPLE

The president of a nonprofit corporation asks a speaker to give the opening address at the organization's fundraising dinner. The president begins his request with the statement, "Although I do not have the budget to pay you, I need a great speaker and you are the best I know." This type of flattery, combined with the opportunity to do something for a worthy cause, makes the request hard for the speaker to turn down.

COUNTER

If the flattery seems sincere, the speaker should express her appreciation. But it is important for her to be able to set the flattery aside when making a decision. If she wants to counter the offer, she can emphasize the importance or value of her speaking skills. A second option would be to ask for some compensation other than money, for example, a free advertisement in the program for the fundraiser.

87. Setting a Time Limit

At any time during a negotiation, either party may *Set a Time Limit* on agreeing to a particular deal point. But remember, you do not have to accept any limits your counterpart sets. In fact, it is a good idea to question all your counterpart's limits. On the other hand, it is also a good idea to go into a negotiation with your *own* limits in mind.

EXAMPLE

You make an offer on a house. The seller counters with a price that is $9,000 higher, and gives you just twenty-four hours to make a decision.

COUNTER

First, you could counter with the tactic of *Asking an Open-Ended Question,* asking why the seller is imposing this time limit. Second, using the tactic of *That's Not Good Enough,* you could tell the seller the time limit is unacceptable and be prepared to walk away. A third option would be *Moving the Deadline.* Tell the seller you cannot respond within twenty-four hours, but will reply in forty-eight hours. This tactic would give you more time to make a better decision. Fourth, you could simply ignore the time limit.

88. Pulling on Your Heartstrings

Once in a while, you may want to remind your counterpart of your long-term relationship or provide some specific details about your circumstances that your counterpart may not be aware of.

EXAMPLE

A corporate customer receives their bank's electronic monthly statement and notes that there is a fifty-dollar charge for a loan payment that was received five days late. The accountant for the corporate customer calls the loan officer at the bank and states, "I have a problem and I need your help. For whatever reason, you received our loan payment five days late. Considering our ten-year relationship, I'm hoping you can make a one-time exception and waive the late charge."

COUNTER

If the bank's goal is to build a long-term relationship with the customer, our recommendation would be to grant the one-time waiver. Adding a *Safeguard* might be wise. The bank could grant the one-time waiver, but specify that if the problem recurs, a fifty-dollar late charge will be imposed.

If the bank's only goal is collecting the fifty-dollar late payment, two counters would be effective. First, the loan officer could tell the customer that the late fees are *Standard Practice or Policy* for the bank and, as such, are nonnegotiable. Second, the loan officer could use *Good Guy/Bad Guy,* offering to ask her manager for permission to waive the fee, and then coming back and saying that her manager refused.

89. The Ambush

Showing up to a negotiation in large numbers, and better yet, unexpectedly, has tremendous impact in a negotiation.

EXAMPLE

A developer goes before the city council to try to get approval for a project. Much to the developer's surprise, more than two hundred citizens show up to oppose the project.

COUNTER

Advance preparation would have made a counter unnecessary in this situation. If the developer had been well prepared, he would have had some idea of the magnitude of his opposition.

Once the *Ambush* has taken place, the developer might request a postponement in the negotiation to have time to regroup and decide on a new strategy. If the developer does not want to postpone—or fails to obtain a postponement—his next option is to try to sell the decision makers on the benefits of his project. He could talk about the number of people his development would employ and the number of tax dollars the project would generate for the city, and express his willingness to work with a citizens' advisory group made up of some of the people who oppose the project.

90. The Field Trip

Anytime you can get your counterpart to leave her office and visit your site or the operation/installation of one of your customers, you obtain leverage. One reason this approach works so beautifully is that it also employs the tactic of *Investing Time* by getting your counterpart to spend time and energy on the negotiation, which raises her level of commitment. A second reason this tactic works is that it gives you the opportunity to show your counterpart how well what you are selling works in real life. This enables your counterpart to envision herself using your product or service.

EXAMPLE

A salesman who sells injection molding equipment invites a potential buyer out to the plant of another customer who is currently utilizing the model of equipment the potential buyer is interested in. The buyer sees that the equipment is working well and the customer is happy with it. As the buyer watches the demonstration, she can actually picture her staff using the equipment.

COUNTER

To protect herself, the buyer needs to make sure she has the ability to walk away from the demonstration without feeling obligated to make a decision on the spot. This ability to walk away will help maintain balance in the negotiation. To make sure she has all the facts, the buyer could plan her own *Field Trip* (possibly to a plant where they are using a competitor's product). The more knowledge she gains about the competition and the product under consideration, the better off she will be. She might even seek out customers who are dissatisfied with the product in question. Any information she acquires will help her gain leverage if she decides to continue negotiating with the first salesman.

91. Jumping on the Bandwagon

One of the most powerful negotiation tactics you can use to sell a customer on the merit of your product is to convince the customer that everyone is using it. In fact, sales are going so fast you can't keep the product on the shelf. The insinuation is that if your counterpart doesn't buy in, he will lose out.

EXAMPLE

If the offer of a free dinner, a weekend's lodging, or a gift certificate has ever succeeded in luring you to a sales presentation for a timeshare, you know how persuasive the sales team can be. Once you have been "captured" by your "personal vacation consultant," you are told how very reasonable this offer is, that you typically spend more on a week's family vacation than you would on a timeshare, that you can trade the share for other property—and on and on. To raise the excitement level and encourage you to commit, the salesperson tells you that the opportunity for you to buy is very limited. Typically, you are in a room where other couples are also meeting with their "vacation consultants." Public announcements are made periodically, stating that various properties are no longer available. The pressure builds and it takes extreme courage not to sign on the dotted line.

COUNTER

The most effective counter is *These Boots Are Made for Walking*. Depending on your tolerance for pain, you can either walk out and forgo the "freebie" or tough it out to the bitter end and collect your free gift. If, on the other hand, you are really interested in the timeshare, you could counter with the tactic of *Good Guy/ Bad Guy* (with your partner playing the bad guy who wants to nix the deal) to gain some leverage, or use *Sweetening the Deal* to try to get something extra thrown in the final package. Another effective tactic is *I'll Think About It and Get Back to You Later.*

92. One Foot on the Dock

This tactic, which is similar to *No More Mr. Nice Guy,* is useful when a counterpart starts making unreasonable demands or causing excessive delays in the negotiation. You start taking punitive action, creating the feeling that your counterpart has *One Foot on the Dock* and the other foot in the boat—and the boat is slowly moving away from the dock.

EXAMPLE

The owner of a commercial building decides to refinance her property since interest rates have dropped significantly. She is negotiating with two banks to try to get the most competitive rate. Using the *Power of Competition,* she keeps gaining concessions from both banks. Finally, the loan officer of one bank, pushed to his limits, tells the building owner that if she does not sign a letter of intent to lock her loan in at 4 percent by Friday at 5 p.m., the rate will go up to 4.13 percent on Monday at 8 a.m.

COUNTER

The easiest counter for the building owner would be to utilize *These Boots Are Made for Walking,* concentrating her negotiations on the other bank she is already working with or opening negotiations with a third bank. A second effective counter would be the *Trade-off Concession*. She could agree to sign the letter of intent at 4 percent if the bank will waive the appraisal and loan fees. Finally, she could employ the *Calling Your Bluff* tactic, telling the loan officer there is no way she can make a commitment by Friday, so if the bank cannot hold the 4 percent interest rate, there is no need to continue the negotiation.

93. Establishing Rapport

Although sharks would debate the value of this tactic, being nice and friendly helps build relationships. A counterpart is much more willing to work with you to create a win-win outcome when he likes and trusts you.

EXAMPLE

You know your negotiation counterpart is an Amiable, so you spend the first five minutes of the negotiation talking about each other's families. Counterparts who are Drivers and Analyticals must make a conscious effort not to leave out this piece of the negotiation puzzle. Amiables respond better to counterparts who take the time to build some rapport.

COUNTER

Some counterparts will go on and on *Establishing Rapport*, never getting to the reason they are meeting in the first place. The best tactic to get things back on track is to ask a question to change the direction of the conversation. A counterpart might eventually tell the Amiable, "It sounds like you had a great vacation last week. Now, as far as this week goes, when were you thinking about implementing the updates to the accounting system?

94. You Pushed Me over the Edge

Once in a lifetime, you are "blessed" with a neighbor or business associate who is truly impossible to deal with. In this rare instance, a special tactic is needed.

EXAMPLE

For two years, Justin puts up with his neighbor's complaints about his dog, his kids, his trees, his car, his choice of music, etc. Justin has finally had enough, and when his neighbor starts harassing him again, Justin says, "I give up! I'll never communicate with you directly again. My next communication with you will be in the form of a letter from my attorney."

COUNTER

The best counter for this nasty neighbor would be to utilize the tactic of *Forgive me, for I Have Sinned* in an attempt to reopen the negotiation. Trying to keep the negotiation open would probably be in the nasty neighbor's best interests, since whenever attorneys get involved in a situation, the attorneys are usually the one ones who come out ahead. A second, more likely tactic for the nasty neighbor would be *Calling Your Bluff*. The neighbor could look Justin in the eye and say, "Great. I look forward to getting your attorney's letter." Although in this example the neighbor seems to be the one who has been the bully for two years, when Justin uses *You Pushed Me over the Edge,* he becomes the bully. A third possible counter for the nasty neighbor would be to try to get closer to the bully (Justin) by asking, "We have been working out our problems for over two years. Why do you see a need to get an attorney involved now?"

95. You Go First

Often in a negotiation, your counterpart will try to "test the waters" by attempting to have you vocalize your outcome first, giving her the advantage of adjusting her offer and perhaps giving less than she was prepared to.

EXAMPLE

I was in the market for a new dishwasher. After researching different models and prices, I was ready to buy. During one shopping trip, I approached a salesman and said, "I have been shopping around and I can get a better price on this dishwasher at XYZ store. I would like to purchase it here but need to know your best price on this model." He asked me, "What price did XYZ quote you?" He wanted me to *Go First* and divulge my bottom line. I stood firm and repeated my question, "What is the absolute best price you can give me?" After a long silence, he finally gave me a price that was below anyone else's price. By forcing him to *Go First,* I'm sure that I got a lower price. Had I gone first, he would have simply matched the price and not beaten it.

COUNTER

In this case, an effective counter would have been to use the tactic of *Calling Your Bluff* and ask for documentation. He could have said that he would consider a lower price if I could show him an ad for the same model at the lower price. Or he could have utilized the tactic of *We've Never Done That Before* and simply state that it is not their policy to match other competitors' prices. If he had given me the best price possible to start with, he could simply stand by that price.

96. Go Easy on Me

There are times when you want the best available product or service but do not want to pay the price that the top product or service commands.

EXAMPLE

In searching for a certified public account, we were given the names of three individuals who were qualified and experienced with our type of business. We interviewed the first two accountants and requested they create a proposal. We scheduled the third account for the last interview because two different people who referred this accountant to us said that she was one of the best, "but very, very expensive." When we met with the third account, we shared the background of how she was referred to us and her associated reputation on price. We ended the meeting by saying, "We would love to work with you, but are not sure if we can afford your fees. Since we are a small business, when you work up the proposal, will you go easy on us?"

COUNTER

In this situation an effective counter could be the *Feel, Felt, and Found*. The accountant might have responded, "I can understand that since you have not experienced the high level of service I provide, you might feel my fees are high. Many of my existing clients felt the same way you do until they discovered that the amount I am able to save them is substantial compared to the fees I charge for my services."

A second tactic that may work well in this situation is to *Lose the Battle to Win the War.* The accountant may have stated something like "I will give you a new-client discount so that you will quickly see that the value gained by my professional services will make the fees seem inconsequential."

97. Blackmail, or I'm Going to Make You Famous

Most people like to see themselves or their company in the media only when the news is good. People and organizations will do almost anything to generate positive publicity and avoid negative publicity.

EXAMPLE

In the past decade, numerous politicians and public figures have fallen from grace because of extramarital affairs or alleged illegal activity.

COUNTER

Assuming that a political figure had participated in an extramarital affair or alleged illegal activity, the most effective counter to this tactic would have been to personally reveal the information before it could be exposed by the media. Exposing information that could be used for blackmail deprives the person making the threat of any benefit of releasing the information, and also gives the person being threatened the opportunity to explain the situation in a better light.

98. Acting the Bully, or Being a "Shark"

One of the most challenging counterparts to deal with is a "shark." Sharklike behaviors include yelling, screaming, swearing, or fist pounding. The tactics sharks and bullies utilize are usually successful because most people would rather give in and retreat—with their shirts still on their backs—than fight.

EXAMPLE

A team of union employees is negotiating a new contract with management. One of the union representatives starts yelling and swearing at the management team members whenever he does not appear to be winning a deal point. His behavior intimidates some of the managers, and they are tempted to give in rather than have the union member continue making a scene.

COUNTER

The most effective way to deal with a shark is to get closer to him, not to retreat. If you show that you are not intimidated, his bullying behavior becomes useless.

In the scenario above, management's representative has four possible counters: (1) He could get up, walk out, and never come back. (2) He could say something like "Most people who negotiate with me do not feel a need to yell, swear, or pound their fists.

I wonder why you feel a need to act this way?" (3) If he knows his counterpart to be a bully, before the discussion even starts he could say, "I have been hoping all week that you will yell and scream like you usually do. Do you promise you will do it for me today?" (4) Finally, if you are really confident and want to have a little fun, you could say, "You know, you frustrate a lot of people when you yell and swear, but it kind of excites me. I love people of passion! Will you do it again?"

These counters work exceptionally well because they help you get closer to the shark or bully. Using them takes confidence, but if you use them well, the shark or bully will yell and swear at others, but most likely not at you.

99. Scrambled Eggs

A counterpart might use the *Scrambled Eggs* tactic to confuse you and your decision-making process. Sometimes facts and figures are used; other times, false information is provided.

EXAMPLE

A salesman is adding up the cost of some furniture. The buyer says she does not want to spend more than $3,000 for the four pieces she is interested in purchasing. The salesman adds up the prices and says the total comes to only $2,800. But when the paperwork is completed, the salesman claims that he has made a $200 error. Once tax and delivery fees are added in, the total is over $3,000.

In a second example, a person selling a car uses facts and figures, such as *Kelley Blue Book* prices, to establish the value of his vehicle. He shares the bottom-line figures with a potential buyer, neglecting to point out that the price he is quoting is for a car with lower mileage. His hope is that the buyer won't ask for proof or a breakdown of figures.

COUNTER

In the first example, the buyer could expose the furniture salesman's tactic, saying that she believes the salesman is deliberately trying to deceive her.

In the second example, the car buyer should ask to see the *Kelley Blue Book* to verify the numbers, and then point out the discrepancy.

In either example, *These Boots Are Made for Walking* would also be effective.

100. I Don't Care

This tactic is generally used by a bully or a shark. At some point in the negotiation, the bully says, "I do not care about what you want" or "*I Don't Care* about you." This behavior has such an emotional impact on the receiving counterpart that it is difficult to respond to. But remember, as always, the counterpart with the least commitment to the relationship holds the most power.

EXAMPLE

A supervisor tells an employee that if he fails to maintain quality standards in his work area, he will be disappointing the team, the rest of the company, and the customers. The employee responds, "*I Don't Care* about you, the team, the rest of the company, or the customers. I just do my job."

COUNTER

The most effective counter in this example is to simply stick to the agenda, which is quality standards in the work area. The employee doesn't have to care as long as he meets the standards. An appropriate response might be, "I need someone in this position who can achieve a ninety-seven percent level of quality. You are not currently achieving this level. Are you indirectly telling me you are not qualified for this position?"

Another tactic, but more difficult, is asking a bigger question: "If you do not care about our team's success or our customers, what basis do we have for a business relationship?"

If this same tactic is used in a business transaction, with one counterpart saying she does not care about the other counterpart or need his business, an appropriate question would be "If you do not care about me or my business, then why are you even taking the time to sit down and talk with me?"

After using either of these counters, the *Silence Is Golden* tactic would be most effective.

The final tactic is one we sincerely recommend you use in every negotiation. When you use this tactic consistently, you'll be amazed at your ability to negotiate win-win outcomes.

101. A Positive Vision

This is an important tactic for you to learn because when you have *A Positive Vision* of the outcome of a negotiation, you will most likely guide its course. If your counterpart does not have a vision, as well as a plan to achieve that vision, he or she will probably be limited to reacting to *your* vision.

EXAMPLE

A contractor is in a dispute with a corporation over the building of its new office, and a meeting is set to discuss cost overruns. The contractor prepares for two weeks and goes into the meeting with a well-orchestrated presentation that is aimed at ending the dispute with a win-win outcome for both counterparts. He visualizes the corporation accepting his proposal. At the meeting, he does a great job of demonstrating how the dispute can be resolved equitably.

Representatives of the corporation enter the negotiation with their primary focus on minimizing their losses in cost overruns. Without their own clear vision of a win-win outcome, they find themselves influenced by the contractor's optimism and commitment to a solution that is favorable for everyone. They accept the contractor's proposal, and both sides come out feeling like winners.

20 Bonus Tactics

1. Picking Cherries

Picking cherries is all about getting the best possible deal on multiple services or products. Once you have established the price based on a complex package, you then single out the part of the package you really want and use the pricing from the bundle to establish the price of a single item.

EXAMPLE

John wants to buy three new snowmobiles for his family. He grew up with snowmobiles and believes it is the best family sport in the winter. He goes to his local snowmobile dealership to purchase three snowmobiles for his family. A sales professional informs him that the price of each snowmobile is $13,500. But, since he is going to be buying three, the salesperson can reduce the price of each snowmobile to $12,000. John is very happy and goes home to share the deal with his family, but John's wife and children are not as excited about the joy of the snowmobile family experience as he is. His wife explains that she is not in support of buying three snowmobiles and feels he should buy only one. That way, other family members can take turns and see if they actually like the sport. John goes back to the dealership and breaks the bad news to the salesperson. He tells the salesperson that his wife has agreed to the $12,000 price and if the salesperson can honor it, he knows he will be able to buy another two.

COUNTER

The salesperson responds by *Never Saying Yes to the First Offer* in hopes of getting something bigger in return. He tells John that he is not able to discount the price of the first snowmobile but he will be able to discount the price of his second and third snowmobile when his family gets excited enough to place the order.

2. Giving Up a Future Draft Choice

There are times in a negotiation where you can gain more by giving up something with the promise and commitment from your counterpart to gain even more at a later point in the relationship.

EXAMPLE

Recently, we had a family discussion about where to go out for dinner. I wanted to go to Applebee's because I love their ribs. My wife and daughters wanted to go to the Souplantation, a wholesome dining restaurant in California, because they love to eat healthy. My son, Barron, wanted to go to In-N-Out Burger. It looked like the girls were going to win and we were off to Souplantation when Barron said, "Wait a second. If we can go to In-N-Out Burger, then I will let you pick where we go out to eat the next two times." Barron was willing to give up a future draft choice for winning a deal point at the present moment.

COUNTER

My daughter Brianne did not miss a beat. First, she *Never Said Yes to the First Offer.* Brianne said, "I hate In-N-Out Burger. For me to agree to go there, then you need to go where we want to go for the next three times." A second counter could be to *Sweeten the Deal.* Brianne could have said, "Barron, if you will go to Souplantation, when we are done, I will buy ice cream at Baskin-Robbins."

3. Acknowledging Emotion

When your counterpart is emotional, angry, upset, or frustrated, it is important to remember that they are blinded by emotion. The strategy in this situation that may work best is to acknowledge your counterpart's emotion and then lead with a question.

EXAMPLE

A management consultant was hired by the CEO of an organization to coach one of his executives. The challenge in this project was a common one. The executive felt it was the CEO who needed coaching and not her. She was angry and frustrated to have to have a coach and was contemplating just resigning from her position. The management consultant thought about the following approaches: agreeing with the executive that resigning was definitely a viable alternative; letting the executive know that if she did not quit, and was uncooperative with the coaching process, she would probably be fired; or let the executive know that she would be happy to coach the CEO but that that was not the goal of this project. Not feeling that any of these strategies was going to build a strong relationship, the consultant *Acknowledged Emotion* and stated, "I can understand how you might feel angry, frustrated, or upset about being asked to work with a coach. In a similar situation, I might feel the same way. Talk to me more about how you feel and specifically how we could make the best out of this opportunity to work together."

COUNTER

In this situation, the executive could counter with a *Conditional No* and state, "I am willing to work with you but right now my schedule is crazy busy and I am unable to focus anytime on my own development until next month. If this can wait thirty days, I will then be ready to move forward."

4. Extreme Security with Full Restitution

One way to maximize leverage during the entire length of a contract is to insert a clause stating that, in the event your counterpart cancels the contract prior to the completion of the entire contract, your counterpart will reimburse you for the total amount of money you have spent, to date. The longer the contract is, the riskier this tactic becomes.

EXAMPLE

A consulting firm and client had come to agreement on a detailed proposal for the services to be delivered during a training contract. In the last revision of the contract, the client inserted a clause that indicated that if the contract was not completed to the client's satisfaction, the consulting firm would compensate the client for the entire cost the client had incurred during the length of the training program, including the hourly compensation rate of the employees attending the training.

COUNTER

The first and best counter to deal with this tactic that could have substantial financial ramifications is to *Say "No" and Stick to Your Guns*. Someone may question, "Why would you want to say 'no' to this tactic if you intend to fulfill your end of the contract?" Even though you are doing everything you are contracted to do, you have no control over what your counterpart is going to do. They may switch contract administrators in the middle of the contract, and this new administrator could be uncooperative. In fact, you find yourself having to invest more funds to make your new contract administrator happy. If the deal point were not in place, you would normally execute your thirty-day cancellation clause and cut your losses. With the full restitution clause in place, however, you would not be able to do that.

If saying "no" is a deal breaker for your counterpart, a trade-off strategy could at least bring some fairness to this lopsided tactic. Tell your counterpart that you are willing to agree to this clause under one condition. They agree to pay you in full for the entire contract if they cancel the contract at any point in the contract's life.

5. Because

A well-known principle of human behavior says that when we ask someone to do us a favor, we are more likely to get that favor if we provide a reason.

EXAMPLE

A consultant calls a client to try to move a training project forward. The consultant tells the client, "I need to find out if you are confirming the week of the twelfth to conduct the training because I have had another client call for those dates, and they need to know by tomorrow."

COUNTER

The client could counter with *If . . . Then* by asking the consultant, "I am going to find it difficult to get you an answer by tomorrow. If you can buy a little more time from your client asking for these dates, then I will be able to get an answer from my division by early next week. Will that work?"

6. Acting Dumb Like a Fox

This tactic, which refers to being cunning while appearing to not be knowledgeable, works well when you are confident you are right, but the counterpart is unwilling to make any concessions, take responsibility, or agree with you. Most times this strategy works well when presented as a question.

EXAMPLE

A CEO has two executives who do not like each other, and refuse to collaborate. The CEO has tried to work with each executive one-on-one but it has not had a positive impact in changing the executives' behavior. In fact, the lack of cooperation, communication, and collaboration continues to get worse between the executives. The CEO decides to *Act Dumb Like a Fox* by bringing the two executives together and asking, "How does it benefit your individual team, the executive team, the company, or our customers when you not only do not work collaboratively, but actively work against each other?"

COUNTER

The executives could *Deflect an Answer with a Great Question.* One executive looks at the CEO and states, "Is it possible that the real problem is that you have done a poor job in clarifying each of our roles, and that is why we have trouble collaborating?" The CEO could, in turn, counter this by *Playing a Broken Record:* "That certainly is possible, but I want to go back and ask you again, what are the benefits to you, your team, the company, or our customers when you do not collaborate?"

7. Three Pros and a Con

One of the challenges in a negotiation is to build trust. It is especially difficult to build trust with a counterpart whose behavioral or negotiation style is highly analytical. To be blunt, people who are highly analytical tend to trust only themselves. The strategy of *Three Pros and a Con* comes into play by telling your counterpart three positive things about your proposal you want them to agree to along with one negative issue that you want your counterpart to realize before they make the decision to move forward.

EXAMPLE

A boat owner makes a decision to sell his yacht. A prospective buyer comes down to the marina to look at the boat. The buyer is highly analytical and asks many questions about every detail of the boat's history and condition. The owner tells the buyer, "There are three great things about this boat. First, it has twin diesel engines with only four hundred hours of use. Second, we have done preventive maintenance to the boat and fixed anything that needed to be repaired. And third, the boat has been professionally washed each week and waxed every six months so the outside is in immaculate condition." The seller goes on to add, "To my knowledge, the only thing that needs to be done on the boat is that the upholstery on one of the couch cushions needs to be repaired."

COUNTER

The buyer uses the tactic of putting a *Safeguard* in place by telling the seller, "You seem really confident about the excellent condition of this boat. I am willing to pay the price you are asking if you are willing to pay for any repairs that are recommended in the engine survey, the sea trial, the haul-out, or the overall boat survey." The boat seller may want to counter this *Safeguard* by putting another safeguard in place: "I am willing to make any recommended repairs up to five thousand dollars."

8. Using the Counterpart's Name

One of the most persuasive tactics in language is the use of someone's name. Although words like *please* and *thank you* are helpful in creating a win-win situation, nothing is more persuasive than using someone's name. The key is to use someone's name within the opening minute of the conversation, and then again as you are coming close to the end your negotiation. If you repeatedly overuse your counterpart's name in a negotiation, you could end up making him uneasy, upset, or angry. Although some people may feel this tactic is silly, our research shows that most often when the counterpart's name is used, you will get a better outcome.

EXAMPLE

You go to a tire shop to buy tires for your car, and have the tires balanced and front end aligned. You ask the person behind the counter for his name: "Thanks, John. I am glad to see you again. I think you helped me last time I was here. My name is Peter. What kind of sale or discounts do you have on four tires for my Ford F150?"

COUNTER

On this particular tactic, there is no effective counter unless the person was repeatedly using your name. In that case, you may *Say "No"* and ask them to stop using your name because it makes you uneasy or uncomfortable.

9. Negotiating for a Third Party

While teaching negotiation at San Diego State University, we created a homework assignment where students had to go to a swap meet, garage sale, or bazaar and buy something to bring back to the class. The caveat was that they could only spend $5, and the only things they could buy were items that the vendor or owner had publicly stated cost $10 or more. The student who brought back the best value to the class would receive a $20 gift card. The advantage of negotiating for a third party (in this case, us) is that it becomes easier to open the negotiation at a higher rate or say no quicker when the counterpart crosses your bottom line (in this case, any product below an asking price of $10 or a selling price of $5).

EXAMPLE

Mary is selling her mountain bike for $20 in her neighborhood garage sale. The bike is in good condition and definitely worth $20. Andrew is interested in buying Mary's bike, but tells her he has been shopping at garage sales all day and only has $5 left to purchase anything. The garage sale is nearing its end time, and $5 is probably going to be the best and last offer Mary will get that day. She rightfully *Says "No,"* but counters back at $10. Andrew *Appeals to St. Teresa,* explaining to Mary that he is buying the bike for a class project and he cannot spend more than $5 or he will fail the project.

COUNTER

Mary counters with a *Conditional No.* She tells Andrew that she cannot sell the bike for that price, but if the bike is still unsold after the garage sale ends for the day, she will sell the bike to him for $5.

10. Establishing an Objective Standard

Since people are involved in every negotiation, emotions will be undoubtedly involved in every negotiation. *Establishing an Objective Standard* helps to help minimize emotion and refocus the negotiation on an objective standard. *Kelley Blue Book,* Edmunds .com, the Consumer Price Index, and the Federal Reserve's discount rate are all examples of objective standards.

EXAMPLE

A client hiring a consultant emails the consultant a contract stating that travel-related expenses are capped at $500 per engagement. The consultant tells the client that a $500 cap is unreasonable because the flight alone will exceed that amount. The client is adamant that $500 in travel-related expenses is the policy, and that all the other consultants abide by it. The consultant researches refundable airfares from three different airlines, calculates the average airfare among the three, and sends all the supporting information to the client. With an objective standard now set, the consultant is on stronger ground in her attempt to increase her travel-related expense amount.

COUNTER

If you don't like your counterpart's objective standard, you could *Ask an Open-Ended Question:* "How is the information you are using relevant to our geographic location?" A second counter could be to trade off with a different objective standard. The client could pull the airfare information from an airline that flies into an airport fifty miles from their office and then recommend the consultant drive the rest of the way to the client's office.

11. Rank-Order

In some negotiations, the counterpart wants everything, making it very difficult to create a win-win outcome. In these types of negotiations, it is helpful to force your counterpart to rank the deal points in order of importance.

EXAMPLE

You are negotiating a contract to provide information technology consulting to a client. The deal points include: price per hour for your services; time when you will start the contract; how long the contract will last; how much general liability insurance you will need to carry; how much time is needed to terminate the contract if she is not happy; and how you will guarantee your work. On every deal point, it is feeling like the client has a deep need to win and does not care much about your goals. You ask them to *Rank-Order* the deal points in order of what is most and least important to them. The client tells you that what is most important to them is that you guarantee your work. With this new information, you are able to put strong guarantees in place and, at the same time, raise your price per hour to meet the client's needs.

COUNTER

The client could *Say No,* because all deal points are important to her. If that did happen, you have the option of employing the counter tactic of *These Boots Are Made for Walking,* with the understanding that if this person is this difficult to work with before you can come to agreement on a contract, she will probably be much more difficult after the contract is finalized.

12. Making the First Offer

Although cases can be made against ever making the first offer, there are situations where it will be to your advantage to do so in order to set a starting point that works to your advantage.

EXAMPLE

Your company has used a data analytics firm for the last five years to help your organization make better, more profitable decisions. The software is highly effective and you pay the software company approximately $50,000 a year. When you started using the company five years ago, there was not much competition. Today there are two competitors in the market who really want your business.

You have met with both competitors and they have provided proposals to furnish the same service for $27,000 and $42,000 annually, respectively. As the procurement manager, you want to go with a competitor to save the company money. The problem is the team members who use the software are committed to the current vendor because they do not want to risk changing vendors or take the time to learn new software. So the procurement manager calls the existing vendor and lets them know he has two competitive bids. And, if they want to keep the business, they will need to repropose the contract in the $25,500 range.

COUNTER

The existing vendor *Says "No"* and then *Asks an Open-Ended Question:* "The competitor is offering you a great price—why are you giving me the option of lowering my price?"

13. Bring Them a Gift

When you give someone something or do a favor for someone, the law of reciprocity tells us that the recipient of your gift will be more motivated to return a gift or favor to you. If you have ever had friends show up around holiday time at your door bearing a gift, then you know the awful feeling of not having a gift to give them in return. The last time this happened at my house, I escorted the guests into the living room, then cornered my wife in the kitchen to ask, "Where is the nice bottle of wine we were given that I can regift to our surprise guests?" No luck—we had drunk the wine, draining my chance to thank my guests with a gift.

EXAMPLE

You show up to negotiate at your counterpart's place of business with coffee and cinnamon rolls. Your counterpart was focused on her negotiation goal, but your kind offer sidetracks her. She responds to your gift by offering to raise the bar and provide treats the next time you meet at your office.

COUNTER

Say thank you and begin your negotiation on a strong note. Or, better yet, let your counterpart know how grateful you are for their gift and *Sweeten the Deal* by offering to buy lunch the next time you meet.

14. Conceding Weird

It is well researched that people are less likely to negotiate decimal numbers (in this case, "weird" numbers) than whole numbers.

EXAMPLE

Mike has advertised his used car for $10,500. Anna is interested: she test-drives the car, has it inspected by a professional mechanic, and decides to offer Mike $9,000 for it. Mike counters back with $10,000. Anna knows that *Conceding Small* in the first round is really important to setting the stage for all future concessions, but she decides she is going to *Concede Weird* by countering with $9,328.12. This offer is going to leave Mike scratching his head, thinking that amount must be all Anna has available in her bank account to buy this car.

COUNTER

Mike decides to *Call Her Bluff* by telling Anna that he cannot sell for that price.

15. Setting the Range

This tactic works best when you have identified your goal (see Chapter 10) and decide to entertain an offer for something that is even beyond your wish.

EXAMPLE

You want to buy a commercial building for your company, and your lender has approved you for $2 million. You have been looking for buildings in the $2 million range, but have not found a perfect fit. Your broker takes you on a tour of one more building listed at $2.5 million, and it turns out it's the perfect one. You know that you have access to more cash if needed to buy this building, but your goal is to buy it for your original $2 million goal. You decide to *Set a Range* and make an offer between $1.7 million and $2.1 million.

COUNTER

The seller *Establishes Rapport* and *Never Says Yes to the First Offer,* declining the $1.7 million offer and countering at $2.25 million. The buyer decides to *Concede Small* and *Concede Weird* at $1,852,412. The deal is finalized at $1,924,000.

16. Turning to a Higher Power

This tactic comes into play when very spiritual or religious people bring their belief in a higher power into the negotiation.

EXAMPLE

I facilitated a salary negotiation between an executive and a CEO. Even though they could not agree on the salary cap, I felt that both sides were committed to the process and we would achieve a win-win. As we sat down to negotiate, the CEO asked if she could start with a prayer. We all bowed our heads and the CEO prayed, "Dear Lord, as we work together to come to agreement on this contract, I hope you will guide us to a reasonable outcome that is a happy medium for both of us. Amen." The executive caved and lowered his salary requirement after that. I was dumbfounded that such a tactic actually worked!

COUNTER

The executive could counter with *That's Not Good Enough,* telling the CEO he prayed she would recognize his true value to the organization and grant him the salary he thought he deserved. He could have also *Said No* and refused the CEO's salary offer.

17. Climbing the Ladder

When we experience a problem with a vendor, supplier, or someone providing us with a service or product, our goal is to get our problem resolved as quickly and efficiently as possible. Many times, the person we are working with to solve our problem does not have the authority to take action, so we have to *Climb the Ladder* to reach the decision maker.

EXAMPLE

Dave bought a first-class ticket for air travel from Los Angeles to Boston with a layover in Dallas. In Los Angeles, the flight is delayed for four hours due to a mechanical issue with the plane, and Dave misses his connecting flight from Dallas and makes plans with the airline to leave the following morning. However, the gate agent can offer him only a business-class seat, without refunding the difference for the first-class seat he originally had. Dave *Climbs the Ladder* and asks for a supervisor who has the power to offer him what he wants.

COUNTER

In this situation, the supervisor could provide a *Trade-off Concession* by upgrading Dave to first class, but on an evening flight. The supervisor may also *Sweeten the Deal* by offering the passenger a $400 voucher, about the amount for the first-class premium, to ease the pain.

18. Dazzling Them with a Great Visual Aid

Being prepared with documentation and visual aids is a great way to demonstrate your knowledge and give you the upper hand in your negotiation.

EXAMPLE

A large consulting firm created a PowerPoint presentation for a prospective client. The first slide read, "Why do clients use our firm?" The second slide was the simple answer, "Positive Results and Increased Profits." Their third slide was a beautiful graph that showed the total dollar value of increased profits all their clients had achieved by implementing their recommendations.

COUNTER

In this example, the client could ask for *Facts and Statistics*, showing specific documentation on how they've helped their clients, and for the consulting firm to provide references.

19. Rain Check

This tactic is appropriate to use when your counterpart is unable to satisfy your request at the moment.

EXAMPLE

Your friend Bob calls you and says, "I have two courtside tickets available for Friday night's game. If you can go, they are yours." Unfortunately, you are traveling this week and so you ask for a

Rain Check: "Bob, this is a fabulous offer and I am so grateful you thought about me when deciding who the tickets should go to. Unfortunately, I am out of town but I would give my left arm to go sit courtside at an NBA game. Is it possible I could take you up on a *Rain Check* for a game later in the season?"

COUNTER

Bob decides an easy counter would be to agree to the *Rain Check*. A second counter could be a *Conditional No:* he won't have the seats available this season, but next season is a possibility.

20. Bait and Switch

Bait and Switch occurs when your counterpart advertises or presents one deal to you, and upon arrival at their location to start the negotiation, they tell you the offer is no longer available and present a second offer that is not as attractive as the first. It is important to note that we encourage readers to be honest at all times and not utilize this tactic, but we will show you how you can counter it if used on you.

EXAMPLE

A hotel chain sends you an email offering you a weekend package that includes two nights' stay, breakfast in the morning, and appetizers in the afternoon along with alcoholic beverage of your choice, all for $299. But when you go online to book the weekend, you are informed that the special-package-price rooms are sold out. The hotel's only rooms available are $179 a night and do not include the free breakfast or the afternoon drink.

COUNTER

There are several counters that may be helpful in this situation. First, you can pick up the phone and talk to the person at the front counter. If this person does not have the power to find you a room in the package deal, *Climb the Ladder* and ask to speak to his boss. If the manager is unable to accommodate your request, then ask for a *Rain Check* for another weekend. Once you get your rain check confirmed, you could let the manager know how disappointed you are that you cannot stay on the original weekend and try to get the manager to *Sweeten the Deal* by upgrading you to a suite.

INDEX OF TACTICS

1. IS THAT YOUR BEST OFFER? 133

Pushing a counterpart to provide his best offer by implying that the offer "on the table" is unsatisfactory.

2. REFERENCING AN EXPERT OPINION 134

Citing the opinion of an authority to gain clout.

3. ASKING A CLOSED-ENDED QUESTION 135

Using a restrictive question to get a direct answer or specific bit of information from a counterpart.

4. ASKING AN OPEN-ENDED QUESTION 136

Using an open-ended question to get more expansive or revealing information from a counterpart.

5. CONCEDE SMALL 137

Sticking to minor concessions in the opening rounds of a negotiation.

6. SHARING BOTH PROS AND CONS 138
Promoting full disclosure by informing a counterpart of both the positive and negative aspects of a proposal.

7. I'LL MEET YOU IN THE MIDDLE 139
Selecting the midpoint between the two counterparts' offers.

8. SILENCE IS GOLDEN 140
Using silence to get a counterpart to talk.

9. SAY "NO" AND STICK TO YOUR GUNS 140
Holding firm on an issue.

10. WOW! YOU'VE GOT TO BE KIDDING! 141
Expressing disbelief to encourage a counterpart to make a better offer.

11. HIGHER AUTHORITY 142
Consulting someone else before accepting an offer.

12. GOOD GUY/BAD GUY 143
Pretending to be on a counterpart's side while consulting another party who keeps vetoing deal points.

13. THAT'S NOT GOOD ENOUGH 145
Saying that the last offer is unsatisfactory to get a counterpart to make a better offer.

14. FACTS AND STATISTICS 146
Using statistics to support an offer or a point of view.

15. TRADE-OFF CONCESSION 147
Getting something in return for everything that is given up.

25. FOCUSING ON THE FUTURE 159
Forcing a counterpart to let go of past issues and look at what's ahead.

26. FORGIVE ME FOR I HAVE SINNED 160
Apologizing for making a mistake or failing to meet all agreements.

27. DEFLECTING AN ANSWER WITH A GREAT QUESTION 161
Asking a question to redirect the conversation.

28. CALLING YOUR BLUFF 162
Telling a counterpart to go ahead and act on a "threat" or "challenge" she has issued.

29. IF YOU WERE IN MY SHOES 163
Asking a counterpart what he would do if the positions were reversed.

30. I FEEL YOUR PAIN 164
Actively listening to a counterpart and empathizing with her feelings.

31. PLAYING A BROKEN RECORD 165
Repeatedly stating a position and refusing to look at options.

32. LAUNCHING A TANGENT 166
Bringing up information unrelated to the negotiation issues.

33. I'LL THINK ABOUT IT AND GET BACK TO YOU LATER 167
Putting the decision off to have more time for consideration.

44. NO MORE MR. NICE GUY 178

Taking back something that has already been agreed to.

45. PERSISTENCE 179

Continually using new and different angles to get a counterpart to agree.

46. ELECTRONIC SHARK IN THE MOAT 181

Setting up "electronic barriers" to avoid negotiating.

47. STALLING FOR CONCESSIONS 182

Delaying a negotiation or decision to encourage the impatient counterpart to make a better offer.

48. MASSAGING A BIG EGO 183

Appealing to a counterpart's sense of power to get him to make a decision.

49. LOSING THE BATTLE TO WIN THE WAR 184

Conceding a deal point or negotiation to win another deal point or preserve a long-term relationship.

50. POWER OF COMPETITION 185

Using competitive bids to put pressure on a counterpart.

51. PUTTING IT IN WRITING 186

Clarifying all the issues involved in a negotiation by specifying the details in writing.

52. FEEL FELT AND FOUND 187

Using empathy to show understanding for a counterpart's concerns and to explain one's own point of view.

81. THE POWER OF CRAZY 215

Doing something irrational to encourage a counterpart to concede deal points just to escape from the behavior.

82. HOW WOULD YOU LIKE TO PAY FOR THAT? 216

Making an offer and assuming a counterpart will accept it.

83. PROVIDING NEGATIVE INFORMATION 217

Using negative information about a competitor to affect a counterpart's decision.

84. THE PERFECT SOLUTION 218

Trying to influence a deal point by offering the ideal way to fulfill all of a counterpart's needs.

85. YOU'LL BE SORRY 219

Moving a counterpart toward an unpleasant outcome, then threatening to push.

86. FLATTERY OR SWEET TALK 220

Appealing to a counterpart's ego.

87. SETTING A TIME LIMIT 221

Imposing a timeline for making a decision.

88. PULLING ON YOUR HEARTSTRINGS 221

Using the power of the relationship with the counterpart to get concessions.

89. THE AMBUSH 223

Showing up to a negotiation in large numbers in hopes of influencing the outcome.

99. SCRAMBLED EGGS 233
Giving a counterpart false information or confusing him with misleading facts and figures.

100. I DON'T CARE ABOUT YOU 234
Using highly emotional language that conveys a lack of concern for the counterpart and/or the deal.

101. A POSITIVE VISION 235
Going into a negotiation with a clear view of a win-win outcome and using that vision to guide the negotiation.

INDEX OF BONUS TACTICS

1. PICKING CHERRIES 237

Establishing the price of a single item by picking out the part of the bundle package you desire.

2. GIVING UP A FUTURE DRAFT CHOICE 238

Giving up something with the promise and commitment from your counterpart to gain even more at a later point in the relationship.

3. ACKNOWLEDGING EMOTION 239

Allowing your counterpart to express her feelings up front.

4. EXTREME SECURITY WITH FULL RESTITUTION 240

Inserting a clause in a contract that protects the time and money you've invested in the project.

5. BECAUSE 241

Giving your counterpart a reason for your request.

6. ACTING DUMB LIKE A FOX 242

Asking a question to which you already know the answer.

7. THREE PROS AND A CON 243

Informing your counterpart of three positives and one negative issue before moving forward.

8. USING THE COUNTERPART'S NAME 244

Using your counterpart's name to build rapport.

9. NEGOTIATING FOR A THIRD PARTY 245

Negotiating on behalf of someone else who has told you the limit that you can spend.

10. ESTABLISHING AN OBJECTIVE STANDARD 246

Utilizing an accepted, reliable resource with your counterpart in your negotiation.

11. RANK-ORDER 247

Listing in order what is most important to your counterpart.

12. MAKING THE FIRST OFFER 248

Telling your counterpart what you are willing to pay to start the negotiation.

13. BRING THEM A GIFT 249

Giving your counterpart something to make them more inclined to return the favor in the future.

14. CONCEDING WEIRD 250

Using a specific, unexpected dollar amount to throw off your counterpart.

15. SETTING THE RANGE 251

Offering your counterpart a specific number range to reach an agreement.

16. TURNING TO A HIGHER POWER 252

Utilizing the power of prayer or a spiritual approach in negotiating with your counterpart.

17. CLIMBING THE LADDER 253

Going above who you are currently negotiating with to work with a person of authority and reach your desired outcome.

18. DAZZLING THEM WITH A GREAT VISUAL AID 254

Using graphics to visually demonstrate your key points and persuade your counterpart.

19. RAIN CHECK 254

When your counterpart is unable to satisfy your request at the moment, you ask for something similar in the future.

20. BAIT AND SWITCH 255

A different offer is presented than what was originally advertised.

ACKNOWLEDGMENTS

The revision of *The Only Negotiation Guide You'll Ever Need* has come together with the help of a great team. First, the team at Peter Barron Stark Companies is the best at challenging our ideas to make them even better. We are especially grateful to Marilyn Rieken for her expertise in proofing our work, ensuring that everything made sense and helping to make us look smart.

Cheers to our agents, Michael Larsen and Elizabeth Pomada. For over fifteen years, they have believed in our team and this project from the very beginning. Their patience, optimism, and unwavering confidence has been an inspiration to us.

Thank you to all our clients and friends who read the book and offered their valuable insights and endorsements. For over twenty-six years, you have supported our work and promoted our books. We are so grateful for both the friendship and business relationship.

Our special thanks to the awesome editorial team at Penguin Random House for their vision, their expertise, and their efficiency in making this project such an enjoyable endeavor.

Finally, thanks to whole the team at Penguin Random House who made this book possible: Tina Constable, publisher; Campbell Wharton, associate publisher; Owen Haney and Ayelet Gruenspecht, publicity and marketing; Nicole Ramirez, production editor; and last, Darren Haggar, who designed a great cover for our book.

BIBLIOGRAPHY

Lynch, Dudley, and Paul L. Kordis. 1988. *Strategy of the Dolphin*. New York: William Morrow & Co.

Navarro, Joe. 2008. *What Every BODY is Saying*. New York: William Morrow Paperbacks.

Nierenberg, Gerard I. 1968. *The Art of Negotiating*. New York: Cornerstone Library.

Nierenberg, Gerard I. 1986. *The Complete Negotiator*. New York: Nierenberg & Zeif.

Nierenberg, Gerard I., and H. Calero. 1971. *How to Read a Person Like a Book*. New York: Cornerstone Library.

Ryan, Kathleen D., and Daniel K. Oestreich. 1991. *Driving Fear Out of the Workplace*. San Francisco: Bard Productions.

Ury, William, and Roger Fischer. 2011. *Getting to Yes*. New York: Penguin Books.

INDEX

ABOUT THE AUTHORS

PETER B. STARK is president of Peter Barron Stark Companies. He travels internationally, delivering keynote speeches as well as training procurement specialists, sales professionals, and other leaders in the art of leadership and negotiation. Speaking more than one hundred days a year, Stark has motivated and inspired thousands of individuals all over the world. Stark holds the prestigious designation of Accredited Speaker from Toastmasters International as well as CSP from the National Speakers Association. This unique combination of awards makes him one of the most sought-after professional speakers in the areas of negotiation, leadership, and change. He has cowritten several books, including *Lifetime Leadership: Leaving Your Legacy, The Competent Leader, Everyone Negotiates, How One Leader Can Make a Difference, Engaged!*, and *Why Leaders Fail and the 7 Prescriptions for Success*. Peter can be reached at (858) 451-3601 or peter@peterstark.com.

JANE FLAHERTY is a senior consultant and trainer for Peter Barron Stark Companies. She has over twenty-five years' experience designing and delivering training programs around the world. She has trained thousands of managers and employees in the areas of leadership, motivation, communication, and negotiation. She specializes in using negotiation skills to resolve conflict, improve communication, and strengthen relationships and teamwork. Flaherty has cowritten several books, including *Lifetime Leadership: Leaving Your Legacy, The Competent Leader, The Manager's Pocket Guide to Leadership Skills, Everyone Negotiates, How One Leader Can Make a Difference,* and *Engaged!* Jane can be reached at (858) 451-3601 or jane@peterstark.com.